The Lucent Library of Historical Eras

Influential Figures of
Ancient Rome

The
Lucent
Library
of
Historical
Eras

Influential Figures of
Ancient Rome

Don Nardo

LUCENT
BOOKS®

THOMSON

GALE

San Diego • Detroit • New York • San Francisco • Cleveland • New Haven, Conn. • Waterville, Maine • London • Munich

On cover: A late seventeenth-century painting
depicts Emperor Trajan addressing the public.

LIBRARY OF CONGRESS CATALOGING-IN-PUBLICATION DATA

Nardo, Don, 1947–
  Influential figures of ancient Rome / By Don Nardo.
    p. cm. — (The Lucent library of historical eras. Ancient Rome)
Includes bibliographical references and index.
  ISBN 1-59018-315-0 (hardback : alk. paper)
  1. Rome—Biography—Juvenile literature. I. Title. II. Series.
  DG203.N369 2004
  920.037—dc21
                          2003003553

Contents

Foreword

Looking back from the vantage point of the present, history can be viewed as a myriad of intertwining roads paved by human events. Some paths stand out—broad highways whose mileposts, even from a distance of centuries, are clear. The events that propelled the rise to power of Germany's Third Reich, its role in World War II, and its eventual demise, for example, are well defined and documented.

Other roads are less distinct, their route sometimes hidden from view. Modern legislatures may have developed from old tribal councils, for example, but the links between them are indistinct in places, open to discussion and interpretation.

The architecture of civilization—law, religion, art, science, and government—as well as the more everyday aspects of our culture—what we eat, what we wear—all developed along the historical roads and byways. In that progression can be traced every facet of modern life.

A broad look back along these roads reveals that many paths—though of vastly different character—seem to converge at a few critical junctions. These intersections are those great historical eras that echo over the long, steady course of human history, extending beyond the past and into the present.

These epic periods of time are the focus of Lucent's Library of Historical Eras. They shine through the mists of history like beacons, illuminated by a burst of creativity that propels events forward—so bright that we, from thousands of years away, can clearly see the chain of events leading to the present.

Each Lucent Library of Historical Eras consists of a set of books that highlight various aspects of these major eras. For example, the Elizabethan England library features volumes on Queen Elizabeth I and her court, Elizabethan theater, the great playwrights, and everyday life in Elizabethan London.

The minilibrary approach allows for the division of each era into its most significant and most interesting parts and the exploration of those parts in depth. Also, social and cultural trends as well as illustrative documents and eyewitness accounts can be prominently featured in individual volumes.

Lucent's Library of Historical Eras presents a wealth of information to young readers. The lively narrative, fully documented primary and secondary source quotations, maps, photographs, sidebars, and annotated bibliographies serve as launching points for class discussion and further research.

In studying the great historical eras, students also develop a better understanding of our own times. What we learn from the past and how we apply it in the present may shape the future and may determine whether our era will be a guiding light to those traveling future roads.

Introduction:
Talent, Energy, and Persistence Leave Their Mark

Ancient Rome's most influential figures—those who shaped Roman civilization the most and brought it its greatest successes—were usually famous both in their own times and in later ages. The vast majority were also gifted in one way or another and found ways of applying their abilities to effect change or persuade people to think a certain way. The first-century-B.C. Roman historian Sallust recognized the natural link between talent and fame. Human excellence, he suggested, was the result of working hard to exploit one's gifts and thereby gain fame. He also pointed out that posterity usually forgets those who lack sufficient talent, initiative, and energy:

> Success in agriculture, seafaring, or building always depends on human excellence. But many [people], who [have been] slaves of gluttony [greed] and sloth [laziness], have gone through life ignorant and uncivilized. . . . It makes no odds, to my mind, whether such [people] live or die; alive or dead, no one ever hears of them. The truth is that no man really lives or gets any satisfaction out of life, unless he devotes all his energies to some task and seeks fame by some notable achievement or by the cultivation of some admirable gift.[1]

Nearly all of the Roman men and women described in this volume fit Sallust's definition of persons of excellence. In this view, they were influential figures because they possessed unusual talents and abilities and applied them with great energy and persistence, leaving their mark on Roman society and often on later societies. The first-century-A.D. scholar Pliny the Elder and second-century physician Galen constitute excellent examples. Both gave themselves fully to their work—Pliny to collecting existing knowledge and Galen to expanding that knowledge through experimentation. And both left behind large bodies of writings that later generations found indispensable.

The poet Virgil and historian Livy, who lived in the first century B.C., were no less talented and hardworking. Each was a highly skilled writer who devoted years of diligent labor to produce an immense literary work tracing Rome's historical roots. Both works glorified Rome in stirring, sentimental tones and made the case that Rome was destined to rule the world. In a very real sense, Virgil and Livy told their countrymen what they wanted to hear, and in the centuries that followed, the image most Romans had of themselves as a great people was the one shaped by these writers.

Similarly, Cato the Elder (second century B.C.) and Cicero (first century B.C.) devoted their own considerable talents to a single noble endeavor, in this case government service. Each was highly intelligent, scrupulously honest, and had the ability to move and persuade others through speaking and writing; each also worked his way up the ladder of public offices to exercise a strong influence over state affairs. Like Virgil and Livy, Cato and Cicero emphasized the importance of Roman tradition and of leaders' responsibility to maintain it. "The Roman state is founded firm, upon ancient customs and on men," Cicero wrote:

> For neither men by themselves . . . nor customs by themselves . . . could ever have sufficed to establish or to maintain, for so long, a state whose empire extends so far and wide as our own. Before our own lifetimes, our traditional customs produced outstanding men, and admirable men, thereafter continuing to maintain those ancient customs and the institutions of their ancestors. [2]

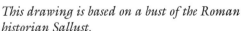

This drawing is based on a bust of the Roman historian Sallust.

9

The Worst Along with the Best

Maintaining revered tradition was a theme stressed by another Roman of extraordinary talent and diligence. After the Roman Republic collapsed in the late first century B.C., Augustus, the first emperor, created a new Roman government to replace it. He made a great show of keeping in place most of the republican institutions, including the Senate and consuls (two administrator generals who served jointly).

However, behind the scenes, Augustus held the real power, which he exercised not tyrannically but constructively. Aided by his capable and personable wife Livia, Augustus worked hard for more than four decades to restore peace, stability, prosperity, justice, and morality to a society that had been severely wounded by the series of civil wars that had brought down the Republic. The influence of the first emperor and empress lasted for generations after their passing.

Dominated by the Temple of Jupiter, Rome's sacred Capitoline hill as it appeared during the reign of the first emperor, Augustus.

Indeed, a century later Roman civilization reached its zenith under a series of emperors who devoted themselves with great zeal to making Augustus's system work for the betterment of the Roman people. Hadrian and Antoninus Pius, two of the five so-called good emperors, oversaw the period lasting from 117 to 161. This was an era of unusual peace, prosperity, and security in the Roman world. Hadrian and Antoninus "persisted in the design of maintaining the dignity of the Empire," the great eighteenth-century English historian Edward Gibbon observed,

> without attempting to enlarge its limits. By every honorable expedient, they . . . endeavored to convince mankind that the Roman power, raised above the temptation of conquest, was actuated [motivated] only by the love of order and justice. [3]

In contrast, one of the most influential of all the figures Rome produced—Constantine I—presided over the Empire in a much less stable, secure, and optimistic era, the early fourth century. The realm had only recently recovered from a series of crises, including its near collapse, some bloody civil disputes, and the most severe Christian persecution in its history. Constantine eliminated his rivals and restored order. Then he set about reversing the fortunes of the beleaguered Christians, granting them toleration, improving their image, and eventually converting to their faith. These efforts, combined with the crusading fervor of a number of church leaders, especially the bishop Ambrose, allowed Christianity to become Rome's official religion by the end of the fourth century.

Including the corrupt emperor Nero (reigned 54–68) and his scheming mother, Agrippina, in the same company as figures of the stature of Cicero, Augustus, and Constantine may at first glance seem strange. Nero, a selfish, egotistical individual with few redeeming attributes, clearly does not fit Sallust's description of a person of excellence. Nevertheless, Nero did leave an indelible mark on Rome and later posterity, mainly because he was in so many ways the opposite of those whose influence was positive and constructive. It might be said that Nero earned everlasting fame by being the exception that proved the rule. In this sense, it is fitting that the worst Rome had to offer be examined along with the best.

Virgil and Livy: Shapers of Rome's Proud Past

The citizens of the Roman Empire looked back with fondness, pride, and a touch of longing at the founding of Rome and the legendary heroes who built and shaped the early Roman realm. These men and women of old were seen largely as ideal figures. In their personal lives they were hardworking, had simple tastes, embraced austerity, and showed contempt for luxury; in their public lives they were honest, devoted to good government and public service, and courageous in defending the homeland against enemies. Moreover, it was thought, these shapers of early Rome were players in a larger drama: Rome's divinely inspired mission to impose order and its superior way of life on the known world. This romantic and inspiring vision of the Roman past became widely accepted and interwoven into the Roman identity—the way the Romans viewed themselves and their place in history.

The shape and tone of this stately vision was largely the work of two men who lived in the final years of the Roman Republic and the first years of the autocratic state that replaced it, the Roman Empire. The older of the two, Publius Vergilius Maro, popularly known as Virgil, was a poet. His *Aeneid* became Rome's cherished national epic. Virgil's younger contemporary, Titus Livius, popularly called Livy, wrote a massive history of Rome that stood as a sort of prose companion to Virgil's epic poem.

Any examination of Virgil's and Livy's careers and their motivations for dedicating their lives to producing these masterpieces must take into account the turbulent and historically crucial period in which they lived and worked. The nearly five-century-old Republic had been rocked by a series of devastating civil wars. The last occurred in the years following Julius Caesar's assassination in 44 B.C. Caesar's adopted son, Octavian, emerged from the ensuing power struggle as sole military and political ruler of Rome in 30 B.C. Soon afterward, the Senate bestowed on Octavian the name of Augustus ("the revered one"). Accumulating a wide array of powers, Augustus remade Rome as an absolute monarchy; however, his long reign, which

A third-century mosaic depicts Virgil attended by two minor goddesses, the muses of epic poetry and tragedy.

came to be called the Augustan Age, turned out to be largely enlightened and constructive. It launched the Pax Romana, a period of nearly two centuries in which the Roman world enjoyed unprecedented peace and prosperity.

Among Augustus's most positive and lasting achievements was his championing of literature. He encouraged wealthy friends to patronize (provide financial and other support for) talented writers; the result was a golden age of literature that nurtured not only Virgil and Livy but also such luminaries as Horace, Ovid, and Propertius. These writers were fortunate to have the support of the emperor and other individuals. They were also lucky that their careers coincided with the return of peaceful times and an era of renewal and stability in Roman society. And they could not help but be affected by witnessing that society undergo a momentous transition from a dangerous, uncertain past to a secure and hopeful future. "It is significant that the greatest writers of this great literary age were all born in republican days," scholar P.G. Walsh writes,

> Like Virgil . . . Livy looked back in shame and anger at the anarchy and savagery of the twenty years preceding Octavian's triumphant return [to Rome] in 29 [B.C.]; those harrowing experiences . . . seem to have been a formative element in the growth of the patriotic literature of the finest creative period ever experienced by Rome. In particular, there is a remarkable correspondence between the spirit animating the first decade of [Livy's history]

and that of Virgil's *Aeneid*. The same central concept of Rome . . . dominates both works. Both conceive the city as divinely founded and . . . guided; both emphasize her imperial mission to establish the Pax Romana throughout the inhabited world.[4]

These works by Virgil and Livy are filled with emotional fervor and adulation for Rome, its people, and especially its heritage. And it is hardly surprising that they became both instant and eternal classics. From their publication at the dawn of the Empire up to early modern times, they consistently shaped Roman and European views of the Roman character and of Rome's fateful foundation and rise to power over the Mediterranean world.

Virgil's Boyhood Influences

The older of the men who produced these influential works, Virgil, was born in 70 B.C. in Andes, a small town near Mantua, in the center of northern Italy, then the province of Cisalpine Gaul. His family was of modest means. His father was a farm laborer and perhaps also a potter, and there were no early indications that this mere farm boy would grow up to be the most famous writer in the world. Only much later, long after the poet's death, did writers attribute omens, miraculous signs of things to come, to his life in an attempt to show that Virgil had always been destined for great things. (Citing such supernatural occurrences was a routine device used by most ancient writers, since the common belief was that the gods always signaled the birth of mortals with extraor-

dinary talents and fates.) Thus, the fourth-century writer Aelius Donatus, who penned the principal surviving biography of Virgil, reported:

> While she was pregnant with him, his mother dreamed that she gave birth to a laurel branch, which struck root when it touched the earth and sprang up on the spot, so that it looked like a full-grown tree. . . . And the following day,

An idealized portrait of Virgil as a handsome young man.

while she was making for the neighboring fields with her husband, she . . . threw herself into a ditch, and disburdened herself by delivering the child. In this manner they say that the child was born, and did not cry, so mild was his countenance; that even then, he gave men no small reason to hope that his birth would prove to be auspicious.[5]

Destiny aside, certain factors in Virgil's childhood on the farm did have a bearing on the development of his worldview and strongly colored his later writings. First, like most rural Romans, he came to love the land and the virtues of agricultural life. As noted scholar Garry Wills puts it:

Romans always had a sharp nostalgia for the fields. Even their worst poets surpass themselves when a landscape is to be described. And all of them associated morality with simplicity, simplicity with the countryside. The city was foul, the country pure.[6]

Certainly, Virgil's love for the Italian land shines brightly in his writings, which praise the simple joys of country life and farm management. "It is a point of honor with him," literary scholar J. Wight Duff points out, "that a reader should learn the make of an old Italian plow, the weather lore, and the rustic festivals of Italy."[7]

Second, Virgil was about eleven when Julius Caesar began governing Cisalpine Gaul (shortly before beginning his famous conquests of Transalpine Gaul, on the far side of the Alps). The young man was fascinated and perhaps a little awed by the stately Julian family that Caesar headed.

Virgil would later give that family a central position in his *Aeneid*, including the glorification of Caesar's great-nephew and adopted son, Octavian.

Establishing a Reputation

As a boy, Virgil could not foresee these developments, of course. He busied himself getting an education, first in the nearby cities of Cremona and Mediolanum (Milan) and eventually, as a young adult, in Rome. His courses included philosophy, rhetoric (the art of persuasive public speaking), medicine, and mathematics. At this time, Donatus says, Virgil was "large in person and stature, with a swarthy complexion." He also had recurrent health problems, "for he commonly suffered from pain in his stomach, throat, and head." In addition, writes Donatus, Virgil was extremely shy: "If perchance someone should spot him in public . . . he would seek refuge in the nearest house, cut off from those who were pointing him out."[8]

The years following Virgil's education remain a bit sketchy. It appears that by 42 B.C. he was back on the farm in Andes, hard at work on his first important set of poems, the *Eclogues*, which extol the virtues of country life. That was the year that the Roman general Mark Antony defeated Caesar's assassins at Philippi (in Greece); the following year Antony's agents seized the farm in Andes, along with many others, for redistribution as rewards to the veterans of the campaign. Distraught, Virgil and his father took refuge with one of the young man's former teachers. (Apparently by this time Virgil's mother had died.)

Virgil's Literary Influences

In this excerpt from his noted study A Literary History of Rome, *the late, highly respected scholar J. Wight Duff discusses some of the myths and literary works that influenced the format and style of Virgil's twelve-volume epic poem, the* Aeneid.

Of the twelve books, the first six—recounting the wanderings of Aeneas—were broadly modeled on the *Odyssey* [by the Greek bard Homer]; the last six—recounting his wars and settlement in Italy—on [Homer's] *Iliad.* . . . The [character of] Medea in the *Argonautica* of [the Greek poet] Apollonius Rhodius was a model for much of the passion of Queen Dido [Aeneas's lover] in Book 4. Lost, as well as extant [surviving], Greek tragedies also affected Virgil's incidents and view of human destiny. . . . With all this borrowing from the Greek, Virgil is one of a national line of [Roman] poets [who were indebted to earlier Greek literature]. . . . The national ring which characterizes the religious as much as it does the political aspect of the *Aeneid,* is due to Virgil's love for the legends of his native land.

Family friends urged the poet to appeal to Octavian, who then shared power with Antony in the alliance known as the Second Triumvirate. Through Octavian's friend, the literary patron Gaius Maecenas, Virgil met and petitioned Octavian. Impressed by the young poet, Octavian used his influence to restore the farm, and Virgil immediately expressed his gratitude in a passage in the first *Eclogue.* "Go feed your cattle as you did before," Octavian is quoted as saying, "and raise your bulls."[9]

Virgil's fortunes had taken a sharp turn for the better on two fronts. First, the *Eclogues* established his reputation as a first-rate poet. Second, he had entered the inner circle of some of the most powerful and in-fluential men in Rome. Maecenas invited the young man into his growing literary circle, the most prestigious in the world, and Octavian awarded Virgil a house in Rome, near Maecenas's, and the use of villas in Naples and Sicily.

On the suggestion of Maecenas, Virgil's next literary project was another set of pastoral verses, the *Georgics.* The poet labored on them for seven years, completing them shortly before Octavian's triumphant return to Rome in 29 B.C. and reading them to Octavian himself at a private gathering. It is clear that the poet already held the man who would soon become known as Augustus in high esteem, viewing him as the war-weary Roman realm's best hope for peace and renewal; the last section of the first *Georgic* contains this poignant prayer:

> Gods of my homeland, heroes of the earth, and Romulus and Mother Vesta [goddess of the hearth], who preserve the Tiber River and Palatine Hill, at the least [I pray that you] do not stop this new champion from putting an era that has fallen down back on its feet. [10]

A Magnificent Statement of the Roman Spirit

The *Georgics* proved extremely popular and from then on Virgil was the most respected and imitated writer in the Roman world. Duff calls him "pre-eminently the poet of his age." [11] This is an apt description because Virgil's writings contain and exemplify all of the major themes that floated through

Virgil (left) reads his Aeneid *to* Augustus, *the empress Livia, and the emperor's sister, Octavia. Overcome with emotion, Octavia has fainted.*

the cultural and literary currents of the era of transition following the fall of the Republic. These included the return of peace and security; the mission of Rome and Italy to rule the world; the beauties of Italy and its fields and farms; praise of Augustus, his family, and his spirits; the revival of religion and traditional Roman virtues and morals; and the glories of Rome's heroic pre–civil war past.

The last of these themes is especially evident in the *Aeneid*, a project suggested to

In this seventeenth-century painting, Aeneas flees the burning Troy with his aged father on his back. The famous Trojan Horse is visible in the distance.

Love's Deadly Wound

Among the many skills Virgil displays in his masterwork, the Aeneid, *is the ability to convey the feelings and yearnings of his characters in a vivid, dramatic manner. An excellent example is this speech (from David West's translation) in which Dido, queen of Carthage, reveals her rising passions for the Trojan prince Aeneas, who recently landed in her kingdom while on his way to Italy.*

The queen had long since been suffering from love's deadly wound, feeding it with her blood and being consumed by its hidden fire. Again and again there rushed into her mind thoughts of the great valor of the man and high glories of his [family] line. His features and the words he had spoken had pierced her heart and love gave her body no peace or rest. . . . She spoke these words from the depths of her affliction to her loved and loving sister: "O Anna, what fearful dreams I have as I lie there between sleeping and waking! What a man is this who has just come as a stranger into our house! What a look on his face! What courage in his heart! What a warrior! I do believe, and I am sure it is true, that he is descended from the gods. . . . I will admit it, Anna, ever since the death of my poor husband . . . this is the only man who has stirred my feelings and moved my mind to waver. I sense the return of the old fires." . . . The tears came when she had finished speaking, and streamed down upon her breast.

Virgil by Augustus himself. One of the poet's strongest skills was his ability to describe and evoke genuine nostalgia for the "good old days," the centuries in Rome's dim past when people were simpler, nobler, and sometimes interacted with the gods. Aeneas, the hero of the *Aeneid,* supposedly lived in this legendary ancient era, hundreds of years before the birth of Romulus, Rome's founder. The story of how Aeneas, a Trojan prince, escaped from the burning Troy (in Asia Minor, what is now Turkey), sailed to Italy, and established the Roman race already existed in scattered myths.

However, both Augustus and Virgil thought that the Roman people (as well as the new regime) would benefit from a detailed, definitive version of the tale, one suggesting that Aeneas had been chosen by the gods to sire a master race with a destiny to rule the known world.

Virgil worked diligently on the great national epic until his death in 19 B.C. Donatus describes his passing:

In his fifty-second year . . . Virgil decided to retire to Greece . . . to put the finishing touches on the *Aeneid.* . . .

While he was getting to know the [Greek] town of Megara, he took sick under the blazing sun. His journey was suspended [and he returned to Italy, but] when he put ashore at Brundisium [in southern Italy] his condition was more serious. He passed away there. [12]

A perfectionist, Virgil did not want his epic to be published unfinished. He had given orders to his literary colleague Varius Rufus to burn the manuscript if this situation arose. Varius could not bring himself to destroy such a masterpiece, however. At Augustus's request, he and another of Virgil's friends, Plotius Tucca, edited the work slightly and published it. Posterity is beholden to these thoughtful men, for the *Aeneid* is one of the greatest literary works produced in ancient times and, as the author had intended, a magnificent, if idealized, statement of the Roman spirit and character.

Piecing Together Livy's Life

While Virgil was the outstanding poet of the Augustan Age, Livy deserves that distinction for prose writing. Livy was not only the most popular historian of his own time but also the most widely read Roman historian of all the ages that followed. It is perhaps ironic, and also vexing, that so little is known about the private life of someone so famous, particularly one who wrote for a living. Unfortunately, none of the many letters he must have penned over the years have survived.

Still, facts gleaned from other sources make it possible to piece together a rough

T.LIVIVS PATAVINVS HISTORICORVM PRINCEPS.IIII.IMPE.TIB.CÆ.OBIIT.

An early modern engraving depicts Livy, Rome's most renowned historian.

sketch of Livy's life. The most widely accepted date for his birth is 59 B.C., although some scholars believe that both his birth and death dates should be five years earlier. There is no debate about where he was born, however: Patavium (Padua), in northeastern Italy. Just as Virgil had been strongly influenced by his childhood on the farm in Andes, Livy's upbringing in Patavium helped mold his own character and outlook. In contrast to the more modern and cosmopolitan Rome, P.G. Walsh points out, the more provincial Patavium

retained much of the strict moral outlook of older days. This conservatism of manners was naturally reflected in its political outlook. . . . Livy's history is imbued with a traditionally pro-republican outlook, and with an emphasis on the strict moral code which regulated the lives of the great republican leaders.[13]

Nothing definite is known about Livy's childhood and education. But he turned out to be an extremely well educated and literate individual, so it can be assumed that at the least he followed the standard steps in a well-rounded male education of that time. This included learning basic reading, writing, and mathematics skills at an elementary school; graduating to a secondary school to study the works of the Greek and Roman poets and historians; and finally receiving instruction in the art of rhetoric from an expert in that field. That Livy studied rhetoric is evident from the way he constructed the many speeches he put in the mouths of historical figures in his great history.

Fame and Remarkable Dedication

Sometime in the late 40s B.C., probably when he was in his late teens or early twenties, Livy began writing. At first he concentrated on philosophy, turning out a number of dialogues, pieces in which two or more characters argue about some disputed topic. For models, he chose the dialogues published by the great republican orator Cicero in 45–44 B.C.

In the years that followed, however, Livy began to focus on history. He moved to Rome, probably shortly after Octavian's de-

feat of Antony at Actium in 31 B.C., in part to study the historical works not available to him in Patavium, but surely also to be as close as possible to the major political developments of the day. At this point, it is likely that he had already decided to produce a large-scale history of Rome leading up to his own day, and it made sense to be in the capital of the known world where he could watch important events unfold.

Fortunately, there is no doubt about Livy's motive in writing his history. It was not, as might be assumed, to give an accurate, unbiased account of actual historical events, the chief motive of modern historians. Rather, as Livy states plainly in the

Livy and other Roman scholars studied scrolls collected in libraries like this one.

work's introduction, his principal goal was to help his readers learn moral lessons by observing both the virtues and failings of past generations. "I invite the reader's attention to the . . . serious consideration of the kind of lives our ancestors lived," he wrote,

> of who were the men, and what the means both in politics and war by which Rome's power was first acquired and subsequently expanded; I would then have him trace the process of our moral decline, to watch, first, the sinking of the foundations of morality as

Pliny the Younger, who mentioned Livy in some of his published letters.

the old teaching was allowed to lapse, then the rapidly increasing disintegration [of the Republic and its lofty ideals], then the final collapse of the whole edifice, and the dark dawning of our modern day when we can neither endure our vices nor face the remedies needed to cure them. The study of history is the best medicine for a sick mind; for in history you have the record of the infinite variety of human experience plainly set out for all to see; and in that record you can find for yourself and your country both examples and warnings; fine things to take as models, [and] base things, rotten through and through, to avoid. [14]

Livy began writing his masterwork, titled appropriately *The History of Rome from Its Foundation (Ab urbe condita libri)*, in 29 B.C. He published most of its original 142 volumes one to three at a time; hence, he became famous after the first few were released, and thereafter people across the known world eagerly anticipated the next installments. Some idea of Livy's popularity is revealed by the first-century-A.D. diplomat and letter writer Pliny the Younger, who asked a correspondent, "Have you never heard the story of the Spaniard from Gades [Cadiz]?" The man was "so stirred by the famous name of Livy," Pliny says, "that he came from his far corner of the earth to have one look at him and then went back again." [15] Another measure of Livy's fame and stature as a writer was that abridged versions of his volumes were popular, too. The first-century poet and humorist Martial list-

Nitpicking Livy

Despite the enormous accomplishment that Livy's history represents, he has often been criticized for his weaknesses. One was surely not a lack of patriotism, although the first-century-A.D. ency-clopedist Pliny the Elder did not see it that way. In his own massive work, the Natural History *(John H. Healy's translation), Pliny nitpicks about what he sees as his predecessor's lack of duty to country.*

[I] confess that I am surprised at Livy, a most renowned author, when he begins one book of his *History of Rome from Its Foundation* as follows: "I have gained enough fame already and I might have settled down to retirement, were it not for my restless mind which feeds my work." Assuredly he ought to have written his history for the glory of the Roman peo-ple, conqueror of nations, and for the Romans' reputation, not for his own glory. It would have been more meritorious to have persevered because of love of the work rather than for his own peace of mind, and better to have done this for the Roman people than merely for himself.

ed some in an inventory of his own books, saying, "Vast Livy, for whom complete my library does not have room, is compressed in tiny skins [pocket versions]."[16] These abridgments also catered to those who lacked either the reading skills or time to tackle the full text.

An even more telling indication of Livy's success is the fact that he was befriended by Augustus himself. We know this because of a brief reference in a work by another great Roman historian, Tacitus. He wrote that, despite the fact that Livy praised Augustus's former enemy, Pompey, the friendship be-tween the historian and the emperor "did not suffer."[17]

Capturing Rome's Romantic Spirit

Livy continued churning out volume after volume of his grand history for some forty-four years, demonstrating a remarkable de-gree of dedication. He was still hard at work on it when he died at Patavium in A.D. 17 (or 12 if the alternate chronology of his life is correct). Unfortunately, of the original 142 volumes, only 35 survive today.[18]

Yet even this partial sample of the work remains a monumental achievement. "Not even in Virgil," writes Duff, "has the great-ness of the Roman character found a more dignified or more lasting monument than in the colossal ruins of Livy's history."[19] One can easily find many faults with the work when comparing it with the more objective and more scrupulously documented tracts of modern historians. Livy did not always use the most accurate sources, for example; nor did he cite many of his sources; nor did he travel to many of the battlefields and other places he mentions to test the accuracy of his sources. He also included a number of mistranslations from other works and freely exaggerated to emphasize a moral point or express his patriotism.

Such criticism aside, Livy's great accomplishment was the creation of a majestic work of sweeping, entertaining prose, a sort of grand adventure story that captured the romantic spirit, if not always the precise facts, of Rome's long and eventful history. He also made that history accessible and appealing to the average person. Despite Livy's weaknesses as a historian, as Duff aptly puts it,

his literary charm stands untouched and untouchable by subsequent researches. His stories may be fabulous, but they fascinate. . . . Livy's history, fictions notwithstanding, is unsurpassed in its fidelity to [Rome's] national character. [20]

Cato and Cicero: Fighting for Traditional Values

Virgil and Livy wrote about larger-than-life figures whose honesty, courage, and devotion to the state shaped the Roman Republic and allowed Rome to fulfill its destiny of ruling the known world. In the pages of Livy's history these characters are often idealized. Yet many were based on real people who did stand for and uphold the values that made the Republic successful for so long. Among those in the long list of republican champions, two of the most prominent were Marcus Porcius Cato, who in the second century B.C. struggled against what he saw as the decay of traditional morals and values, and Marcus Tullius Cicero, who in the following century waged a valiant but losing battle to save the Republic from collapse.

Austerity, Frugality, and Duty to Country

The first of these towering figures, Cato,[21] was born in 234 B.C. in Tusculum, a small town at the base of the rolling Alban Hills, southeast of Rome. Perhaps significantly, this was the heart of the region that Virgil and Livy identify as the home base of the Roman founders, Aeneas and Romulus, and thereby the fountainhead of Roman tradition. Indeed, an abiding respect for ancient tradition was the hallmark of Cato's character; throughout his life, he staunchly defended old-fashioned Roman values, including austerity, honesty, the virtues of agricultural life, and the intrinsic worth of the Latin language (in an era in which almost all literature of worth was in Greek).

Cato displayed these qualities, which so many Romans viewed as admirable, from an early age while growing up on a wealthy farming estate. According to his chief ancient biographer, the first-century-A.D. Greek writer Plutarch, "Ever since his early youth he had trained himself to work with his own hands, serve as a soldier, and follow a sober mode of living, and hence he possessed a tough constitution."[22] In the dimly remembered days of the early Republic, many Roman men would have fit this description. However, by Cato's day, such simple-living individuals were in much shorter supply. "A man who observed the ancestral custom of working his own land," Plutarch continues,

> who was content with a cold breakfast, a frugal dinner, the simplest clothing, and humble cottage to live in, and who actually thought it more admirable to renounce luxuries than to acquire them—such a person was conspicuous by his rarity. The truth was that by this date the Roman Republic had grown too large to preserve its original purity of spirit, and the very authority which it exercised over so many realms and peoples obliged it to adapt itself to an extraordinary diversity of habits and modes of living.[23]

Not surprisingly, therefore, the conservative and austere Cato stood out from his peers, even as a young man. He gained further notoriety while serving in the army during the Second Punic War (218–201 B.C.), the titanic conflict against the empire of

A sixteenth-century Italian painting depicts Cato in Renaissance attire.

Carthage (centered in North Africa), in which victorious Rome gained control of the whole western Mediterranean sphere. As Plutarch tells it,

> [Cato] served in his first campaign when he was seventeen years old. . . . In battle he was a formidable fighter,

who stood his ground resolutely and confronted his opponents with a ferocious expression. . . . When he was on the march he used to carry his own armor and weapons on foot [instead of using donkeys or slaves, as most soldiers did], and would be followed by a single attendant who looked after his food and utensils. [24]

The Moral Crusader

In 204 B.C., as the great war neared its end, Cato served as quaestor (an official in charge of finances) for the noted general Scipio (later called "Africanus"), who was planning to invade North Africa. Cato was disturbed in that office: He thought that Scipio led too

lavish a lifestyle and was corrupting the native simplicity of his soldiers by paying them too much. Returning to Rome, Cato spoke out against Scipio and tried, in vain, to get him relieved of his command.

After the war, Cato decided to enter public service. He dutifully began the customary climb up the ladder of public offices expected of young men aspiring to be leading politicians. Having already served in the lowest ranked of these offices, quaestor (which qualified him to become a senator), Cato was elected aedile, one of two officials in charge of maintaining public works and buildings, in 199 B.C. Higher offices came in rapid succession. In 198 B.C. he served as governor of the island province of Sardinia (lying off Italy's western coast), and in 195

The Qualities of a Good Farm

Cato's farming manual, On Agriculture, *written in the early second century B.C., has the distinction of being the oldest surviving Latin prose work. In the following excerpt, Cato discusses some of the factors that make a farm prosperous.*

[The farm] should have a good water supply. It should be near a thriving town or near the sea or a river where ships go up or a good and well-traveled highway. . . . See that it has good buildings. . . . If you ask me what sort of farm is best, I will say this: One hundred *jugera* [about 63 acres] of land consisting of every kind of cultivated field, and in the best situation; [of these,] the vineyard is of first importance if the wine is good and the yield is great; the irrigated garden is in the second place, the willow plantation in the third, the olive orchard in the fourth, the meadow in the fifth, the grain-land in the sixth, forest trees to furnish foliage in the seventh, the vineyard-trained trees in the eighth, [and] the acorn wood in the ninth.

B.C. the people elected him consul. After his consulship was over, Cato was appointed to a second governorship, this time of the province of Farther Spain, where he won distinction for putting down a large rebellion.

In the wake of Cato's service in Spain, bitter feelings between him and Scipio, which had been simmering for years, boiled over. Each man tried to discredit the other but, thanks in part to his eloquence as a speaker in the Senate, Cato prevailed. A corruption trial badly damaged the considerable reputation of Scipio and his family.

Conversely, Cato's own reputation as a moral crusader grew apace, and soon he became a candidate for censor, a prestigious state official charged with maintaining public morality. The Romans, Plutarch wrote,

believed that a man's true character was more clearly revealed in his private life than in his public or political career, and they therefore chose two officials [the censors] . . . whose duty it was to watch, regulate, and punish any tendency to indulge in [corrupt or disreputable] habits and to depart from

A Renaissance painting shows the battle of the Ticinus River in which Scipio fought as a young man. Cato later bitterly opposed Scipio.

the traditional . . . way of living. [The censors] had the authority to . . . expel a senator who had led a vicious or disorderly life. They also carried out . . . a general census of property, [and] kept a register of all citizens.[25]

Cato was elected censor in 184 B.C. and quickly showed that he intended to enforce the powers of his office to the letter. He sternly denounced a number of senators and other well-to-do individuals for immoral behavior and excess luxury and of setting a bad example for the rest of the populace. In one celebrated case, Plutarch reports, Cato expelled a senator named Manilius "on the ground that he had embraced his wife by daylight in the presence of his daughter."[26] It comes as no surprise that the man whom posterity remembers as "Cato the censor" became widely disliked by the upper classes. The common people, however, admired Cato so much that they raised a statue in his likeness.

"Carthage Must Be Destroyed!"

Cato also attempted to serve the Roman people by educating them about their history and the proper way to run a farm. His long, encyclopedic history of Rome, covering events from the era of the kings to his own time, became known as the *Origines (Beginnings)*. Unfortunately, this first major history of Rome written in Latin is lost. However, in Cato's day and the century that followed, the work exerted a strong influence on new generations of Roman historians.

Cato throws North African figs on the table of the Senate to emphasize that Carthage remains prosperous and a threat to Rome.

Another of Cato's works, *On Agriculture*, which has survived, advises well-to-do absentee landlords on how to manage a country farming estate; it also contains much fascinating information about the rural customs and lore of the time.

Still another way Cato influenced his countrymen was through his powerful oratory. A memorable example of this was the stand he took against Carthage. Since their defeat in 201 B.C., the Carthaginians had faithfully honored the terms of the peace treaty they had signed with Rome. However, this was not enough for Cato, who still nurtured a deep hatred for the old foe. In 153 B.C., when he was in his eighties, he visited Carthage and was both surprised and angry to see it thriving and happy. In Cato's view, it would only be a matter of time before the

Carthaginians once again posed a threat to his own nation. Returning to Rome, he began lobbying for a third Punic war that would rid the world of Carthage once and for all. Thereafter, Cato ended every speech he made, no matter what the topic, with the words *"Delenda est Carthago!"*—"Carthage must be destroyed!"

Cato got his wish, but he did not live long enough to see the destruction he was instrumental in bringing about. He died in 149 B.C., the same year Rome launched its last war against Carthage. Three years later the Romans literally wiped that city from the face of the earth. However, this brutal act did not end the dangers the Republic faced, as Cato had hoped. He could not have foreseen that the direst danger the Roman state now faced would come not from the outside but from within.

The Young Cicero

It was during the early manhood of Rome's last great republican champion, Cicero, that this dire danger—powerful Roman generals leading their own personal armies against the government—began to manifest itself. Marcus Tullius Cicero was born on January 3, 106 B.C., on a well-to-do farming estate near Arpinum, about sixty miles southeast of Rome. His father, Marcus Cicero, may have operated a fuller's shop (a sort of laundry); the elder Cicero also helped manage the estate. It is uncertain what crops were grown in the fields in which Marcus Tullius and his younger brother Quintus romped as boys. Anthony Everitt, author of a recent biography of Cicero, speculates:

For wealthier landowners, olives and grapevines were popular. Grain would have been sown on the plain below Arpinum, and grass fields would have supported sheep, goats, and oxen. Timber was a valuable commodity and it is likely that willows were cultivated by the river to provide baskets . . . for transporting agricultural products. Doubtless, there would have been an orchard and vegetable garden near the house. [27]

A more definite fact about the Cicero household was that its men were very proud of their family name, so much so that they were willing to endure periodic ridicule over it. According to Plutarch,

Cicer is the Latin word for chick-pea, and Cicero's distant ancestor no doubt got the name because he had a kind of dent or nick at the end of his nose like the opening in a chick-pea. Certainly Cicero himself . . . is said to have given a spirited reply when he first entered politics . . . and his friends thought that he ought either to drop or change his name. He said that he was going to do his best to make the name of Cicero . . . famous. . . . [Later] when he made an offering to the gods of some silver plate, he had his first two names, Marcus and Tullius, inscribed on the plate and then, by way of a joke, told the craftsman to engrave a chick-pea instead of the third name. [28]

Whether the elder Cicero reacted to remarks about the family name with such humor is unknown. More certain is that he had high ambitions for his sons and made sure they attended the best local school. The name of the school has been lost, but the memory of Marcus Tullius's stellar performance there has survived. "His natural abilities made him altogether remarkable," Plutarch writes,

> and won him such a name and reputation among the other boys that their fathers used often to go to the schools and see Cicero with their own eyes to observe [his] quickness and intelligence. . . . He was the sort of person who takes gladly to every branch of learning and who rejects no aspect of literature or of education. [29]

A Blaze of Fame

It was clear to all, Cicero included, that he was destined for a distinguished professional career, in either the law or politics. Both jobs appealed to him, and both required excellent oratorical skills. So, after graduating secondary school, Cicero traveled to the Greek island of Rhodes to study rhetoric with the most respected speech teacher in the known world—Apollonius Molo. Soon afterward, the greatest lawyer of the day, Mucius Scaevola, tutored the young man in the legal profession.

Fresh from these studies, Cicero wasted no time in entering the practice of law and rapidly made a name for himself. "He was ambitious by nature," Plutarch says. "So when he took up his work as an advocate [lawyer], it was by no means slowly or grad-

ually that he came to the top. He blazed out into fame at once and far surpassed all his competitors." [30] His first big case came in 80 B.C., when he defended Roscius, a man who had supposedly killed his own father. The advocate prosecuting Roscius was close to Cornelius Sulla, then dictator of Rome (and

Cicero delivers a speech from the speaker's platform in Rome's main Forum.

the first Roman general to march his troops on the capital), and Sulla was eager to see the accused man convicted. Therefore, Cicero showed considerable courage in taking the case. But after winning it, he decided that caution would be more prudent than bravery and took a long trip to Greece and Asia Minor. Although it was clear to all that he was trying to avoid Sulla's wrath, Cicero cited health reasons for the trip, later writing,

> I was thin in those days, and my physical condition was by no means robust. . . . In fact, I had the type of physique for which hard work and lung strain are regarded as practically fatal. . . . My friends and my doctors urged me to give up pleading [cases] altogether. . . . That is why I left [Rome].[31]

Less than two years later Sulla died and Cicero returned to Rome and resumed his legal career. Not long afterward, the young man felt the time was right to enter politics, too, and he eagerly began the ascent up the same ladder of offices Cato had climbed. Cicero was elected quaestor in 75 B.C., entered the Senate a year later, served as aedile in 69 B.C., and gained the office of consul in 63 B.C.

The success Cicero experienced during these years was based largely on the high regard the Roman voters had for him. The average citizen saw him as a champion of old-fashioned values, an honest, unselfish man who truly cared about the welfare of the state and the people. This was exactly the image Cicero wanted to convey, and his

writings suggest that it was not mere show. In his great work of moral philosophy, *On Duties* (44 B.C.), for example, Cicero asserted:

> Those who are about to take charge of public affairs should . . . first fix their gaze so firmly on what is beneficial to the citizens that whatever they do, they do with that in mind, forgetful of their own advantage. . . . The management of the Republic is like a guardianship, and must be conducted in the light of what is beneficial not to the guardians, but to those who are put in their charge.[32]

Hero and Exile

Cicero's character and leadership abilities met their staunchest test yet shortly after he won the consulship. A crisis loomed when the man who had lost the election to Cicero—a disgruntled aristocrat named Catiline (Lucius Sergius Catilina)—sought revenge by scheming to kill the new consuls and take over the government. Catiline and his cronies were not discreet enough, however, and Cicero got wind of the conspiracy. At a Senate meeting, with Catiline himself present, Cicero delivered a speech, one of his greatest, that daringly exposed the plot. "In the name of heaven," he roared at Catiline,

> how long will you exploit our patience? Surely your insane activities cannot escape our retaliation forever! Are there to be no limits to this audacious, uncontrollable swaggering? . . . Look at

Cicero (on the Senate floor) rails at Catiline, who sits alone, shunned by his fellow senators. The conspirator soon escaped and died in battle.

this meeting of our Senate . . . [and] see the expressions . . . of every one of these men who are here! . . . You must be well aware that your plot has been detected. Now that every single person in this place knows all about your conspiracy, you cannot fail to realize it is doomed. . . . Now, Catilina, your hopes must obviously be at an end. The darkness of night no longer avails to conceal your [treachery]. . . . All your schemes are more glaringly evident to us than the light of day.[33]

Nervous and desperate, Catiline reacted by hurling insults at his accuser, but the other senators shouted him down. The traitor fled and tried to rally the small army of followers he had gathered, but Cicero's fellow consul, Antonius, smashed them a few months later in a pitched battle. Catiline died fighting and thereby escaped the hand of the executioner. His leading accomplices in Rome were not as fortunate, however. Cicero convinced the Senate to have the remaining conspirators strangled to death in their cells without the benefit of trials, which was their right by law. For the moment, the rescue of the government made Cicero a hero. People cheered him in the streets and hailed him as "Father of His Country."

But the adulation was short-lived, for denying the conspirators their civil rights had been a mistake. Cicero and other defenders of the republican system had political enemies, the strongest among them the rising political star Julius Caesar, the noted

A bronze bust of Julius Caesar. Though enemies, he and Cicero respected each other.

an official who could influence the passage of laws and also veto them. He managed to push through a new law that outlawed anyone who caused the death of a Roman citizen without a trial, a move obviously directed at Cicero's execution of the Catilinian conspirators. Cicero had no choice but to go into voluntary exile, and he soon ended up in Greece. There, Plutarch writes, "he remained for most of the time miserable . . . keeping his eyes fixed, like a distressed lover, on [the direction of] Italy."[34]

The Spirit of the Republic

In the months that followed, Clodius burned Cicero's house in Rome and continued trying to damage his reputation. But these efforts failed, as Cicero remained popular in many quarters. When Clodius's term as tribune ended in 57 B.C., the Senate promptly passed a resolution allowing Cicero to return home. It also ordered his house to be rebuilt at public expense.

In a very real sense, however, the Rome that Cicero returned to was a different place than the one he had left. Riots and street fights, many involving the troublemaker Clodius, had recently ravaged the capital. Meanwhile, the three triumvirs continued to wield influence, consistently challenging the Senate's authority and interfering with its efforts to run the government. Even after the triumvirate fell apart, an even greater threat replaced it. The advent of military generals amassing their own armies to challenge the state reached crisis proportions in 49 B.C.; Caesar returned from his conquests in Gaul at the head of a large force

general Pompey, and the influential millionaire Marcus Crassus. In 60 B.C. the three men united to form the First Triumvirate and used their combined powers to intimidate the government and get their way. Cicero remained a thorn in their side. To silence him, Caesar encouraged another of the orator's enemies, a shady character named Clodius, to step up his attacks on Cicero. Clodius was then serving as tribune,

of battle-hardened troops and launched a civil war against Pompey and the Senate. In the face of these developments, Cicero grew more and more disillusioned. Finally, in 46 B.C., after Caesar had won the war and declared himself dictator of Rome, the great orator retired from politics, feeling his voice was no longer effective.

However, the situation changed once more when Caesar was assassinated in 44 B.C. Believing there was hope for his beloved Republic after all, Cicero reentered politics. Unfortunately for him, Mark Antony, the general who now attempted to fill the power vacuum left by the dictator's demise, detested the orator. Cicero delivered several powerful speeches denouncing Antony (the *Philippics*), calling him a gangster, spiritual bankrupt, drunk, and other unsavory things.

Once again, a burst of patriotic fervor had caused Cicero to miscalculate, for Antony soon retaliated with brutal force. In the winter of 43 B.C., Antony joined forces with Octavian and Marcus Lepidus in the Second Triumvirate, and Cicero's name

Cicero Consoles His Family

Cicero's career, accomplishments, and writings are so enormous and important that overviews often overlook his family life. In 79 B.C. he married Terentia, a well-bred young woman from a wealthy family. They had a daughter, Tullia, who died in 45 B.C., causing Cicero extreme sorrow, and a son, also named Marcus Tullius, who later served as consul alongside Octavian. Following is an excerpt from a letter (quoted in Selected Political Speeches of Cicero*) Cicero wrote to Terentia, Tullia, and Marcus in November 58 B.C., while he was in exile in Greece.*

Many people write to me and everybody tells me about how unbelievably brave and strong you are being, Terentia, and about how you are refusing to allow your troubles . . . to exhaust you. How unhappy it makes me that you with your courage, loyalty, honesty, and kindness should have suffered all these miseries because of me! And that our darling daughter Tullia has been plunged into such wretchedness because of her father. . . . And what can I say about our son, Marcus, who . . . has known the bitterest grief and sorrows. . . . I cannot write about the rest of it—my tears would get the better of me, and I do not want to reduce you to the same condition. I only say this: if our friends remain true to us, there will be no lack of money. . . . Keep well, and send me messengers so that I know how things are going and how you are all getting on.

topped Antony's list of enemies to eliminate. Cicero was murdered at his country house at Astura (about fifty miles south of Rome). By Antony's order, soldiers nailed the great man's head and hands to a platform in Rome's main square.

Cicero left behind not only the legacy of a brilliant political career but also a huge body of writings, most of which have survived. These include fifty-eight lengthy speeches, more than eight hundred letters, and some two thousand pages of philo-

Antony's henchmen apprehend Cicero as he tries to flee to Greece. They cut off his head and hands, which were publicly displayed in Rome.

sophical works. Thanks to these, and the many things written about him by other ancient writers, more is known about Cicero than any other figure of antiquity. In retrospect, a portrait emerges of a multitalented man with a dedication to good government and a spirit of humanity far greater than any of his opponents. That such a person should suffer so brutal a death is sad. Yet even sadder was the realization of his friends and supporters that he had embodied the spirit and ideals of five centuries of republican government and that, for all intents and purposes, the Republic had died with him.

Augustus and Livia: Rulers of a New Rome

As Cicero and others of the old guard of republican Rome passed away or gave up fighting the inevitable, the Republic crumbled. In its place rose a new, more autocratic Rome, a government and realm that came to be known as the Roman Empire. It was largely the creation of Octavian, renamed Augustus. Although Augustus refrained from using the title of emperor, history viewed him as Rome's first, for he wielded enormous power and influence. Yet he administered this great authority mostly through traditional republican institutions and on the whole used it in constructive ways. As a result, his beneficent reign became the model against which those of his successors were measured.

At the same time, Augustus's wife, Livia, became a model in her own right. She was the most powerful, independent, and influential woman Rome had ever seen. In a union that lasted fifty-two years, she privately advised and influenced her husband and managed their enormous household (which included more than a thousand relatives and other dependents). More importantly, she found a workable balance between the traditional, domesticated image of women and the newer, more liberated one, setting an example for later upper-class wives and daughters. In his recent biography of Livia, scholar Anthony Barrett elaborates:

> The Roman woman was by tradition devoted to her husband . . . and spent her time and energies on the efficient run-

ning of her household, a paragon of impeccable virtue, a perfect marriage partner. . . . [However,] by Augustus's day the image of the Roman woman as a mere wife and mother was in practice becoming difficult to sustain, at least among the upper classes. . . . Roman women had by then acquired the right to inherit, own, and bequeath property and had attained a level of independence still unmatched in many modern-day states. . . . In the eyes of the world, Livia succeeded in carrying out her role of model wife to perfection. . . . [Yet with the creation of the Empire] she found herself . . . in an unparalleled situation, with no precedent to guide her. She was the first "first lady"—she had to establish the model to emulate, and later imperial wives would to no small degree be judged . . . by comparison to her. . . . [She managed] to display the grand dignity expected of a person very much in the public eye, combined with the old-fashioned modesty of a woman whose interests were confined to the home. [35]

Octavian and Caesar

Thus, both Augustus and Livia showed considerable restraint in wielding the extraordinary powers and prestige they held. In his younger days, however, when he was still called Octavian, he had displayed considerably fewer scruples about using force to achieve his goals.

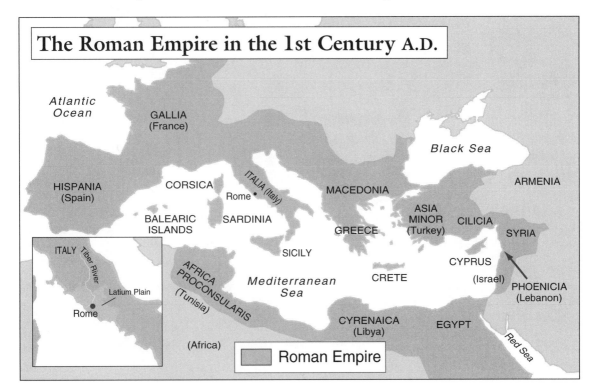

The Roman Empire in the 1st Century A.D.

Gaius Octavius the Younger was born in Rome in 63 B.C., the year in which Cicero saved the Republic by foiling the conspiracy of Catiline. In his youth, Octavian did not fit the stereotype of a man with an ambition to conquer and rule. Unlike his great-uncle, the tall, imposing, and forceful Julius Caesar, Octavian was short, slight of build, and prone to sickness. "His body is said to have been marred by blemishes of various sorts," wrote the first-century Roman historian Suetonius. "He had a weakness in his left hip, thigh, and leg, which occasionally gave him the suspicion of a limp . . . [and he] survived several grave and dangerous illnesses at different periods."[36]

Despite the boy's frail constitution, Caesar took a liking to him, and the two periodically spent time together during the great civil war that Caesar launched against Pompey in 49 B.C. At one point, Caesar invited Octavian to join him on a campaign in Spain. Too sick to leave with his uncle, the young man eventually caught up, man-

Caesar is assassinated in the Senate, near Pompey's statue. Following the murder, Octavian traveled to Rome to collect his inheritance.

aging a dangerous journey that showed considerable resolve and courage. According to Suetonius, Octavian

> followed [Caesar] with a very small escort, along roads held by the enemy, after a shipwreck, too, and in a state of semi-convalescence from a serious illness. This action delighted Caesar, who . . . soon formed a high estimate of Octavian's character. [37]

Caesar became so fond of and impressed by the young man, in fact, that in September 45 B.C. he made him his heir. Also, that winter, hoping to prepare Octavian for a successful political career, Caesar sent him to Greece to study under the renowned scholar Apollodorus of Pergamum. It was there, a few months later, that a messenger gave Octavian the news that Caesar had been assassinated on March 15, 44 B.C.

Outmaneuvered by a "Mere Boy"

Now nineteen, Octavian returned to Rome to collect the inheritance that was due him as Caesar's legal heir. But he was immediately confronted with an obstacle, namely Mark Antony, Caesar's chief military associate, who was presently the chief strongman in Rome. Not a great judge of character, Antony made the mistake of underestimating Octavian and treating him with contempt. "Antony was at first inclined to despise Octavian as a mere boy," Plutarch wrote,

> and told him that he must be out of his mind, adding the warning that a young

man who possessed few influential friends and little experience of the world would find it a crushing burden to accept the inheritance and act as Caesar's executor. . . . Antony for his part did everything possible to humiliate him. [38]

Octavian's reaction to this shabby treatment was to turn the humiliation back on Antony by deftly outmaneuvering him. The younger man quietly got the backing of both a small army of Caesar's troops and most of the senators. Antony was unprepared and proceeded northward to gather troops of his own. The Senate then decided to send the two consuls and Octavian against Antony. They defeated him twice in a row, but the consuls were killed and the wily Octavian now demanded to be made consul in their place, despite the fact that he was under the legal age to serve in that high office. At first the senators balked, but when the young man marched his new army on Rome they realized that they, too, had been outmaneuvered and grudgingly acceded to his demands.

In the months that followed, Octavian continued to demonstrate an unusual degree of shrewdness. He reasoned that Antony would raise larger armies to use against him and that another strong general, Marcus Lepidus, could also prove troublesome. So Octavian followed the example Caesar had set with the First Triumvirate and offered his rivals a deal. According to Plutarch,

> Antony, Lepidus, and Octavian met on a small island in the middle of a river, and there their conference lasted for

three days. They found no difficulty in agreeing on a great range of subjects, and they divided the rule of the whole world between them as easily as if it had been a family inheritance.[39]

The triumvirs first ruthlessly eliminated most of their chief political enemies, including the great Cicero. Then they headed for Greece, where the leaders of the plot to kill Caesar—Brutus and Cassius—awaited with an army. In two pitched battles fought late in 42 B.C. near Philippi, Antony's and Octavian's forces were victorious and Brutus and Cassius chose suicide over capture.

Despite these triumphs, the triumvirs continued to encounter problems. Octavian and Antony squabbled and Antony's first wife, Fulvia, led a failed rebellion against Octavian. The two men made temporary amends in October 40 B.C. by signing the so-called Treaty of Brundisium, which granted Octavian most of Rome's western lands and Antony the eastern ones.

Enter Livia

Octavian also had to deal with intermittent warfare with Pompey's son, Sextus Pompeius, one of the opponents the triumvirs had tried but failed to eliminate three years before. The same year as the Treaty of Brundisium, Octavian tried to offer an olive branch to the younger Pompey through a dynastic marriage. One of Pompey's relatives, a well-to-do young woman named Scribonia, became Octavian's bride and bore him his only child, Julia.

This arranged marriage was not a good one. And in any case, it did not last long be-

This drawing is loosely based on surviving busts of Livia.

cause the following year (39 B.C.) Octavian met Livia in Rome. Her full name was Livia Drusilla; she was born in 58 B.C., when Octavian was five. Her father, a prominent nobleman named Marcus Livius Drusus Claudianus, had fought against Octavian and Antony at Philippi and joined Brutus and Cassius in suicide after their defeat. When she met Octavian, Livia was married to Tiberius Claudius Nero, who had served as quaestor a few years before. In 42 B.C., she had borne Nero a son, Tiberius (the future emperor), and she was now pregnant with their second child (Drusus).

Livia's delicate situation did not deter her relationship with Octavian. By all accounts the two fell deeply in love almost immediately and, despite the scandal that ensued, began living together. Without further ado, Octavian filed for divorce from Scribonia (on the same day she gave birth to Julia) and Nero agreed to divorce Livia without a fuss, probably concluding that opposing a triumvir would be foolhardy. In fact, when Nero died a few years later, his will entrusted the guardianship of Tiberius and Drusus to Octavian. With the divorces out of the way, Octavian and Livia married in January 38 B.C.

After the marriage, Octavian and Livia tried to put the scandal behind them and thereafter projected the image of the model Roman couple. Livia enjoyed some special privileges that other women did not. In 35 B.C., for example, Octavian arranged for her (along with his sister, Octavia) to receive the status by which an attack on her person was the same as an attack on the state; this status also allowed Livia to control her own money and property. Still, for the first several years of their marriage she kept a low public profile and busied herself mainly in the traditional domain of Roman women— domestic matters. Despite the family's wealth, she made many of her husband's and sons' clothes, and she saw to the welfare of not only Tiberius and Drusus but also Julia and in time Julia's four children and various grandchildren and in-laws.

Rule of the First Citizen

At least part of the reason Livia remained in her husband's shadow in the early years of

Octavian and Agrippa (on horses) survey the scene following their victory at Actium. Defeating his rivals made Octavian the strongest figure in Rome.

their union was that, during this period, he was frequently preoccupied with crucial political and military affairs; for a woman to involve herself in such matters would at that time have appeared unseemly. First, the triumvirate finally fell apart. Octavian and Antony pushed the weaker Lepidus aside and then opposed each other in another civil war, in which Antony had the support of Egypt's Queen Cleopatra VII. In September 31 B.C., Octavian, aided by his friend and chief military adviser, Marcus Agrippa, defeated them at Actium, in western Greece.

With all of his rivals dead or neutralized, Octavian was the strongest political and military figure in the Mediterranean world; even the Senate, once the leading organ of government, dared not oppose him. The question was whether he would use his great power and influence for selfish goals, as most dictators do, or in more constructive ways. Fortunately for Rome, Octavian chose the latter. As for his method of rule, he was wise enough to avoid looking like an absolute monarch, which in many ways he was, realizing that many Romans would find this unacceptable. For one thing, during the civil wars he had promised to restore the old republican traditions and values. Also, the lesson of his great-uncle's failed dictatorship

Democracy or Dictatorship?

In his Roman History, *Dio Cassius asserts that, while contemplating how to restructure the Roman government, Augustus asked for the advice of his trusted friends Gaius Maecenas and Marcus Agrippa. Maecenas advocated a benign dictatorship, which Augustus did establish. Agrippa's argument, which was rejected, was for democracy. The following is an excerpt of that argument.*

The fact that . . . democracies are greatly superior to monarchies, is shown by the example of Greece [especially Athens during the period of 500 to 300 B.C.]. So long as the peoples of Greece were subject to monarchies, they achieved nothing of consequence, but once they began to live under popular rule, their fame spread throughout the world. . . . But why need we refer to the examples set by other peoples, when we have our own at home? We Romans at first lived under a different form of government [a monarchy]. Then, after enduring many harsh experiences, we longed to obtain our liberty. After we had won it, we rose to the position of proud authority which we enjoy today. . . . At any rate, the ancient Romans hated tyranny so passionately . . . that they even declared that form of government [monarchy] to be accursed.

was fresh in his mind. As noted scholar A.H.M. Jones points out, Caesar

> enjoyed fully as much military and popular support [as Octavian did], but was assassinated by a group of senators when he made it plain that he was never going to resign his dictatorship. There was an immensely strong sentiment among the upper classes . . . against absolute rule. They had been educated in the tradition of the . . . expulsion of the kings . . . the wise rule of the Senate, and the republican form of government was sacrosanct [sacred] to them.[40]

Thus, Octavian cloaked his dictatorial powers in the trappings of the old republican system. He knew that the Roman people were exhausted from decades of war and uncertainty, and he was confident that, to acquire peace, they would be willing to accept the leadership of one powerful individual, on the condition that he was efficient, just, and maintained Roman tradition.

Using this approach, Octavian, whom the Senate renamed Augustus ("the revered one") in January 27 B.C., began assembling a new Roman governing system, which became known as the Principate, or Empire. (The term *Principate* means "rule of the Princeps"; Augustus insisted on being called Princeps, or "first citizen," rather than emperor.) In his *Res gestae,* a summary of his deeds composed in old age, Augustus claimed that "after I had put an end to the civil wars, having attained supreme power by universal consent, I transferred the state

This idealized portrait of Augustus was fashioned several years after his death.

from my own power to the control of the Roman Senate and people."[41] This verbal sleight of hand was code for his shrewd consolidation of a wide array of republican offices and powers, always in a seemingly legal and above-the-board manner. In time, Augustus held most of the authority formerly wielded by the consuls, Senate, tribunes, and censors and quietly influenced who would be candidates for the consulship and other state offices that were now largely ceremonial. All the while, he reinforced his image as a simple, modest man of the people. "May I be privileged to build firm and lasting foundations for the Government of the State," he said on one occasion.

> May I also achieve the reward to which I aspire: that of being known as the author of the best possible Constitution, and of carrying with me, when I die, the hope that these foundations which I have established for the State will abide secure. [42]

The Augustan Age

It remains unclear to what degree these noble words were sincere and to what degree they were motivated by political expediency; probably they were both. What is certain is that during Augustus's forty-four years in power he did rule in a just, constructive manner and ushered in the long period of peace and prosperity that became known as the Pax Romana.

Not surprisingly, considering the era of war and destruction that had recently ended, the main themes of Augustus's reign were reform, healing, renewal, and the restoration of lost traditions and values. Perhaps the most obvious aspect of renewal took the form of a series of large-scale public building programs. Though it was the biggest and certainly the most important city in the Empire, Rome was old, dirty, and unattractive, with many badly built apartment buildings that sometimes collapsed, causing death and suffering. "Aware that the city was architecturally unworthy of her position as capital of the Roman Empire," Suetonius states,

> Augustus so improved her appearance that he could justifiably boast: "I found Rome built of bricks; I leave her clothed in marble." . . . Among his very numerous public works [were] his Forum [town square] with the Temple of Avenging Mars . . . and the Temple of Jupiter the Thunderer on the Capitoline Hill. . . . Some of Augustus's public works were undertaken in the names of relatives, such as the colonnade and basilica of his grandsons Gaius and Lucius, [and] the colonnades of his wife Livia and sister Octavia. . . . Also, he improved the approaches to the city, repaving the Flaminian Way . . . at his own expense. [43]

Augustus also reorganized the military. He created a standing, or permanent, army, taking care to provide the troops adequate rewards and pensions to keep them from showing more allegiance to their generals than to him and the government. He constructed two large navies as well, along with several smaller navies to defend the provinces. In addition, he organized a special force of elite troops—the Praetorian Guard—to guard his person and see that his policies were implemented.

Among the Princeps's other accomplishments were the formation of a police force and fire brigade for the capital city; major administrative and tax reforms; and

Rome's main Forum as it appeared in the early Empire. Augustus also erected a new forum named after himself.

generous financial and moral support for the arts, especially literature. The Roman people came to respect, rely on, and even love him. When Augustus died on August 19, A.D. 14, at the age of seventy-six, the outburst of grief, both public and private, was greater than for any past leader. His fu-neral procession was immense, as hundreds of thousands of people marched or lined the streets. According to the second-century Roman historian Dio Cassius, when Augustus's coffin was placed on the funer-al pyre, soldiers tossed onto it the decora-tions he had awarded them.

Praise for the Dead Augustus

In his history of Rome, Dio Cassius includes a speech delivered at Augustus's funeral by his stepson and successor, Tiberius. (Ancient historians rarely had access to the exact words of such speeches, so they largely paraphrased them, as Dio does here.)

He [Augustus] could by virtue of . . . the armed strength and the money at his command have proclaimed himself the supreme and sole ruler. . . . Yet he refused, and . . . first brought back to health and then returned to your keeping the whole system of [republican] government. . . . He provided for [the Roman people] public works, distributions of money, games, festivals . . . an abundance of the necessities of life, and security, not only from wrongdoers and foreign enemies, but even from the acts of the gods. . . . How too could I forget to mention a man who lived his private life in poverty and used his wealth only for public service; who treated himself with austerity but others with lavish generosity; who took upon his own shoulders every hardship and danger for your sake. . . . This, then, was why you had good reason to make him your leader and the father of the people, why you honored him with so many distinctions . . . and why you finally . . . declared him to be immortal. And so it is right that we should not mourn for him, but that while we now return his body to nature, we should glorify his spirit for all time as that of a divine being.

A modern rendering of Livia attending her husband on his deathbed.

After this the centurions [army officers] took torches . . . and set fire to the pyre from below. So it was consumed, and an eagle released from it flew aloft to bear the emperor's spirit to heaven. When these ceremonies had been completed, all the others departed, but Livia remained on the spot for five days. . . . Then she had his bones gathered up and placed in his tomb.[44]

Augusta

The three main legacies Augustus left behind were property, power, and prestige, and his will stipulated that Livia and Tiberius were to be the main beneficiaries. Livia received a third and Tiberius the rest of the estate. Tiberius got most of the power because Augustus had formally adopted him and groomed him to be his successor. However, Livia was granted a good deal of prestige, as the will also directed that she should receive the title of Augusta, or "mother of the emperor." This gave her an important symbolic role in public life, which otherwise only a handful of priestesses enjoyed. Among the other honors and privileges Livia received were the right to sit with high priestesses in the theater and to have her image appear on coins. The Senate even debated whether to bestow on her the title of *parens patriae,* or "Parent of the Country." The new emperor vetoed this proposal, however. According to Tacitus, Tiberius "was jealous and nervous, and regarded this elevation of a woman as derogatory to his own person."[45]

Indeed, Tiberius worried that Livia might accumulate enough power and prestige to challenge his own authority. He therefore began to avoid her and did everything he could to keep her from amassing any more prestige. Suetonius writes:

Although [Tiberius] did occasionally need and follow Livia's advice, he disliked people to think of him of giving it serious consideration. A senatorial decree adding "Son of Livia," as well as "Son of Augustus," to his honorific titles . . . deeply offended him. What is more, he often warned Livia to remember that she was a woman and must not interfere in affairs of state. He became especially insistent on this point when a fire broke out near the Temple of Vesta and news reached him that Livia was directing the populace and soldiery in person. At all events he visited her exactly once in the last three years of her life.[46]

When the emperor retired to the isle of Capri (near the Bay of Naples) in the 20s, Livia remained in Rome. There she wielded considerable influence by helping friends on trial gain acquittal, advancing the careers of deserving young men, sponsoring the restoration of public buildings, patronizing poetry competitions, and undertaking other generous acts. Livia remained ever busy until she

Livia and Her Son at Odds

In this excerpt from Suetonius's biography of Tiberius (in Lives of the Twelve Caesars*), the historian describes the animosity the emperor felt for his mother, Livia, in the years following Augustus's death.*

Tiberius quarreled openly with his mother. The story goes that she repeatedly urged him to enroll in the jurors' list the name of a man who had been granted citizenship. Tiberius agreed to do so on one condition—that the entry should be marked "forced upon the emperor by his mother." Livia lost her temper and produced from a strongbox some of Augustus's old letters to her commenting on Tiberius's sour and stubborn character. Annoyance with her for hoarding these documents for so long, and then spitefully confronting him with them, is said to be his main reason for retiring to [the remote isle of] Capri. At all events he visited her exactly once in the last three years of her life, and only for an hour or two at that.

fell ill and died in 29 at the venerable age of eighty-six. Tiberius did not attend the funeral. The ceremony was a simple one, after which Livia's body was placed beside the bones of Augustus in his tomb. Rome's first emperor and empress, both unique, larger-than-life characters, now assumed places of honor in the collective memory of the Roman people, to be revered in centuries to come alongside Romulus, Rome's founder, and Brutus, father of the Republic.

Nero and Agrippina: The Corruption of Power

In the eyes of history, the fifth Roman emperor, Nero, and his mother, Agrippina, have become legendary for their selfishness, cold-bloodedness, and corruption of the great power and trust vested in them as emperor and queen mother. He has often been portrayed as cruel, extravagant, murderous, and sexually perverted; she has been depicted as all of these things as well as a schemer and poisoner.

It must be emphasized, however, that the lens of history often tends to distort and exaggerate the personalities and deeds of flamboyant and sensational public figures, making them seem better or worse than they really were, and royal or noble families are always grist for the gossip and rumor mills. It is certain that Nero and his mother were innocent of at least some of the disreputable acts attributed to them. When examined dispassionately, for instance, the evidence does not support the popular charge that Nero started the great fire of A.D. 64. Nor has it been proven that he and Agrippina engaged in incest.

Similarly, the accusation that Agrippina poisoned a number of men to further her political schemes remains unproven. As modern biographer Anthony Barrett points out, wealthy, influential noblewomen were frequently suspected of poisoning in the early years of the Empire, especially those in Augustus's family (the Julio-Claudian dynasty, to which Nero and Agrippina belonged). Even Livia, Augustus's wife, who was known for her generosity and kindness, endured rumors that she poisoned people to further her aims. That does not mean that Agrippina was not a poisoner. She may well have been. But as Barrett says, "Even in our own day, with the help of science . . . police investigation and a systematic court procedure, it is notoriously difficult to determine the truth in poisoning cases." [47]

Similarly, the fact that some of Nero's bad reputation was undeserved does not whitewash the portion that *was* deserved. There is no doubt that Nero was self-absorbed, a murderer, and in general a ruthless, though weak, ruler, one of the worst to occupy the throne during the Pax Romana. In the words of his recent biographer Richard Holland:

> In little more than half a century since the death of Augustus, his carefully balanced system of government seemed in imminent danger of degenerating into some form of oriental tyranny. . . . [Nero] lacked any of the recognized qualifications for holding down the position of Princeps in the Augustan constitution. [48]

Fortunately for Rome, the "danger" Nero and Agrippina posed to the new imperial system was short-lived. First, he brutally removed her; then, the army and upper classes conspired to remove him.

Wavering Family Fortunes

Actually, the traumatic events of Nero's misrule and removal would never have occurred in the first place had it not been for Agrippina's ceaseless efforts to place him in a position of power. As a brief overview of their political rise reveals, Nero was not originally part of the expected imperial succession. Agrippina was born Julia Agrippina (or Agrippina the Younger) in A.D. 15, the year after her great-grandfather, Augustus, died. Her birthplace was the Roman military colony that later became the city of Cologne, on the Rhine River, the border between Roman Gaul and Germany. Her mother was Vipsania Agrippina (or Agrippina the Elder, daughter of Julia, Augustus's daughter, and Marcus Agrippa), her father Germanicus Julius Caesar (grandson of Augustus's sister,

Nero's image on Roman coins inspired this modern drawing of the emperor.

Agrippina's Magnificent Outfit

The lives, appearances, and habits of Roman and other ancient figures are often, of necessity, pieced together from small passages from many contemporary writers. The following description of Agrippina decked out in a magnificent outfit is an eyewitness account by Pliny the Elder, recorded in his Natural History.

I have seen Agrippina, the wife of the Emperor Claudius, at a [public] show where he was presenting a naval battle, seated by him, wearing a military cloak made entirely of gold cloth. Gold has long been woven into the fabric called Attalus cloth; this was invented by the kings of Asia.

Octavia); one of her brothers, Caligula, became the third emperor.

Thus, Agrippina hailed from an impressive lineage of wealthy, influential people, including a mother and great-grandmother (Livia) known for being strong but admirable women. Exactly why and how Agrippina grew into a strong but much less admirable woman is unknown. The process may have begun when in 28, at the age of thirteen, she married Gnaeus Domitius Ahenobarbus, a rich aristocrat with a reputation for dishonesty and cruelty. In the next few years the young woman faced repeated bouts of grief, embarrassment, and fear. First, her mother and one of her brothers were banished by the reigning emperor Tiberius on suspicion of plotting against him; both died in exile, the mother by starvation, the brother by either murder or suicide. Then another of Agrippina's brothers died in prison.

The family's fortunes improved in 37 when Tiberius died and Caligula succeeded him. At first Caligula showed favor to his sister, making Agrippina an honorary vestal virgin (a great honor, since the vestals, who maintained the state hearth, were the most prestigious priestesses in Rome). In that same year Agrippina gave birth to her son Nero (then Lucius Domitius Ahenobarbus) in the small seaside town of Antium, about fifty miles south of Rome. The manner of the birth was later seen as an omen of the corruption to come. According to Pliny the Elder,

Nero, who throughout the whole of his rule was the enemy of mankind, was born feet first. It is Nature's way for a man to be born head first, and man's custom to be carried out for burial feet first. [49]

Nero was only two when the family was once more beset with misfortune. In 39,

The vestal virgins attend Rome's sacred hearth. Caligula, the third emperor, made his sister Agrippina an honorary vestal.

Caligula, who had begun his notorious descent into mental instability and tyranny, banished Agrippina, claiming she was involved in a conspiracy to overthrow him. (It remains unknown whether the charge was true.) The following year Nero's father died. This was a serious setback for Agrippina, since she needed to be married to a wealthy, influential man in order to promote her son's interests with any success.

Marriages of Convenience

Returning to Rome after Caligula's assassination in 41, Agrippina married a nobleman, Gaius Passienus Crispus, who had served as consul in 27. The details of the marriage are unknown. Passienus died about two years later, and some suspected Agrippina of poisoning him, although, as Barrett asserts, there is no proof "that Passienus's end was anything other than natural."[50]

No one knows when Agrippina set out to place her son in the imperial succession. What is certain is that her next marriage, in 49, was to her uncle, Claudius, the fourth emperor. Claudius already had a son—Britannicus, who was three years younger than Nero. Yet the following year, Agrippina, aided by one of the emperor's close advisers, the freedman (freed slave) Pallas, secured Nero's legal adoption as Claudius's second son. According to Tacitus:

[Pallas] pressed Claudius to consider the national interests and furnish the boy Britannicus with a protector. . . . The emperor was convinced. Echoing the ex-slave's arguments . . . he promoted Lucius Domitius Ahenobarbus [who thereafter was known as Nero Claudius Caesar] above his own son. [51]

Tacitus also reports that at the same time Agrippina received the title of Augusta. She was only the second woman to receive this honor (the first being Livia) and the first to receive it while her husband was still living.

Agrippina was finally in a position of tremendous influence, as Claudius was easily swayed and manipulated by wily, ambitious women. [52] In the next few years Agrippina used her newfound power to eliminate those she viewed as political enemies or potential rivals to her and her son. Eventually, she turned on the emperor himself. According to ancient sources, with the aid of various palace accomplices she poisoned Claudius to

Agrippina's Long-Term Impact

In his excellent biography of Agrippina, noted scholar Anthony Barrett provides this insightful commentary on her long-term impact on Rome's imperial community.

[Agrippina] represents an essential stage in the evolution of the imperial system, in the attempt to give a formal definition to the political role open to women of ability and energy. She did not change the hardened attitudes of her contemporaries, but she did define what Romans were willing to tolerate. Her experiment [in manipulating the system] may have been a failure but it was not without its long-term effects. It can surely not be a coincidence that she was the last woman to play a dominant role in Roman political life for a century and a half. Later generations of imperial wives and mothers who might otherwise have entertained aspirations to power clearly took to heart the bitter lesson that Agrippina learned when, in A.D. 59, she was beaten and hacked to death by her son's hired assassins.

death in October 54. And much to her delight, her sixteen-year-old son, Nero, ascended the throne, becoming the fifth ruler of the Roman Empire.

High Hopes for a Young Ruler

At first, most of the senators and other high-placed Romans believed that the new emperor would prove himself a moderate and responsible leader. Suetonius writes:

> Nero started off with a parade of filial dutifulness: giving Claudius a lavish funeral, at which he delivered the oration himself. . . . As a further guarantee of his virtuous intentions, he promised to model his rule on the principles laid down by Augustus, and never missed an opportunity of being generous or merciful, or of showing how affable he was. He lowered, if he could not abolish, some of the heavier taxes. . . . If asked to sign the usual execution order for a felon, he would sigh: "Ah, how I wish that I had never learned to write!" . . . Once, when the Senate passed a vote of thanks to him, he answered: "Wait until I deserve them!" . . . He [also] gave an immense variety of entertainments—coming-of-age parties, chariot races in the Circus [Maximus], stage plays, [and] a gladiatorial show. [53]

At least some of the good behavior Nero exhibited in the early part of his reign may have been the result of the influence of his tutor and adviser, the witty philosopher and writer Lucius Annaeus Seneca. It was Seneca who had written the boy's first official speech to the Senate, as well as the moving oration delivered at Claudius's funeral. Seneca apparently did whatever he could to put the young emperor on the right path, as both a man and a ruler.

Unfortunately, these efforts failed, as Nero grew increasingly brutal and despotic as time went on. First, he killed his stepbrother, Britannicus, to ensure that the youth would never be able to challenge him for the throne. (The boy was poisoned so powerfully that his skin turned dark, and to divert suspicion of foul play his body was coated with a light-colored substance.)

Matricide

Next, Nero turned on his own mother, a singular piece of ingratitude considering that she was the person most responsible for putting him in power. In his first year or so as emperor he seems to have trusted and admired her. "Nero turned over all his public and private affairs to Agrippina's management," says Suetonius. "And she and he often rode out together through the streets in her litter." [54]

As for why the young emperor decided to rid himself of Agrippina, most historians speculate that he grew increasingly irritated with her criticisms and attempts to control him. "No matter how valuable Agrippina might be to Nero," Barrett suggests,

> it was almost inevitable that she would find it difficult to maintain her predominant position of influence and power. . . . Nero was a very young man,

A modern drawing based on one of Agrippina's surviving busts.

with an inflated opinion of his own talents and abilities, and it would have been natural for him to want to show that he was capable of establishing his own, independent role. . . . Nor did Agrippina's attitude help. . . . She tried to dictate his choice of friends, and . . . [he] was offended by her . . . constant criticism of his behavior. . . . A mother who constantly reminded him that he was an immature youth who needed to adhere to her advice . . . would soon wear out her welcome. [55]

The celebrated matricide, which took place in March 59, was a painfully lengthy affair that resembled a sort of dark comedy of errors. Nero "tried to poison her three times," Suetonius claims, "but she had always taken the antidote in advance." Next, his henchmen

> rigged up a device in the ceiling of her bedroom which would dislodge the panels and drop them on her while she slept. However, one of the people involved in the plot gave the secret away. Then he [Nero] had a collapsible boat designed which would either sink or have its cabin fall in on top of her. [56]

This plan failed, too. The boat did sink, but Agrippina was a strong swimmer and she made it safely to shore, where a crowd gathered and escorted her to her country villa. According to Tacitus, the news that the queen mother had survived the shipwreck sent Nero into a panic: "Half-dead with fear, he insisted she might arrive at any moment. 'She may arm her slaves!' he cried. '"She may whip up the army, or gain access to the Senate . . . and incriminate me!"'" [57] Finally, he sent soldiers to finish her off. It is said that when they drew their swords, Agrippina resolutely pointed at her womb and ordered them to strike there, the place that had nurtured her ungrateful son. Then, writes Tacitus, "blow after blow fell, and she died." [58]

Nero's Other Victims

Britannicus and Agrippina were not Nero's only victims. In 53, before becoming emperor, he had married Octavia, Claudius's daughter. But five years later, now sitting on the throne, Nero became infatuated with

Nero the Mugger?

In his biography of Nero (in Lives of the Twelve Caesars*), Suetonius claims that the notorious emperor derived perverse pleasure from disguising himself and mugging innocent strangers, a charge that, if not false, is likely exaggerated.*

As soon as night fell, he would snatch a cap or a wig and make a round of the taverns, or prowl the streets in search of mischief—and not always innocent mischief either, because one of his games was to attack men on their way home from dinner, stab them if they offered resistance, and then drop their bodies down the sewers. He would also break into shops and rob them, afterwards opening a market at the palace with the stolen goods . . . auctioning them himself, and squandering the proceeds. During these escapades he often risked being blinded or killed—once he was beaten almost to death by a senator whose wife he had molested, which taught him never to go out after dark unless an escort of bodyguards was following him at an unobserved distance.

Poppaea, the beautiful wife of a close friend. The affair went on until 62, when Nero divorced Octavia and imprisoned her on a false charge of adultery, after which he married Poppaea. Then the new imperial couple had Octavia killed. However, in what now seems a touch of poetic justice, Poppaea soon suffered a miscarriage and bled to death. (Rumors spread that Nero had thrown a temper tantrum and kicked her in the abdomen, but they remain unsubstantiated.)

The Roman people also suffered under Nero. Although in the early part of his reign he had reduced taxes, he now raised them. He also unfairly confiscated the lands of a number of wealthy men. In addition, Nero came to ignore Seneca and other responsible advisers and turned instead to Ofonius Tigellinus, the brutal and ambitious commander of the Praetorian Guard. Tigellinus, likely out of self-interest, only encouraged the emperor's increasingly self-indulgent and conceited behavior.

One way such behavior manifested itself was in Nero's distorted vision of his own creative talents. To his credit, he was a big supporter of the arts. However, he came to see himself as a divinely gifted poet, musician, and actor and frequently performed in public, which did not help his image or reputation. Society viewed actors as socially disreputable characters; in addition, evidence suggests that Nero possessed only minimal musical talents and that he bored the audiences who were required to attend his recitals. "No one was allowed to leave,"

Suetonius reports, "however pressing the reason." [59] He adds that some people tried to escape by pretending to die so that their bodies would be carried out of the theater.

Nero's Role in the Great Fire

Considering all the unsavory or misguided acts attributed to Nero, it is ironic that he became most infamous for a crime he did not commit. In July 64, a devastating fire swept through the capital, destroying about two-thirds of the city. According to Tacitus:

> It began in the [wooden seats of] the Circus [Maximus]. . . . Breaking out in shops selling inflammable goods, and fanned by the wind, the conflagration instantly grew and . . . there were no walled mansions or temples, or any other obstructions, which could

The great fire of A.D. 64 destroyed nearly two-thirds of Rome. Though Nero was suspected of starting the blaze, it is unlikely he was involved.

arrest it. . . . Of Rome's fourteen districts only four remained intact. Three were leveled to the ground. The other seven were reduced to a few scorched and mangled ruins.[60]

Tacitus says that the emperor quickly launched relief efforts. He turned his own guards into firefighters, opened many public buildings and even his private gardens to accommodate the homeless, and brought loads of food in from neighboring towns to distribute to the destitute. Afterward, he allocated large sums of money to rebuild devastated districts and introduced a strict new building code that greatly reduced the risk of future fires.

"Yet these measures, for all their popular character," Tacitus points out, "earned no gratitude. For a rumor had spread."[61] The essence of the rumor was that Nero had ignited the blaze himself, partly to clear away

A modern reconstruction of Nero's Golden House. The giant statue of the emperor mentioned by the historian Suetonius stands in the alcove at upper right.

The Golden House

Suetonius describes Nero's Golden House and its surrounding parklands in this excerpt from the historian's biography of the emperor in Lives of the Twelve Caesars.

The entrance-hall was large enough to contain a huge statue of himself, 120 feet high; and the pillared arcade [covered walkway] ran for a whole mile. An enormous pool, like a sea, was surrounded by buildings made to resemble cities, and by a landscape garden consisting of plowed fields, vineyards, pastures, and woodlands—where every variety of domestic and wild animal roamed about. Parts of the house were overlaid with gold [giving the place its name] and studded with precious stones and mother-of-pearl. All the dining-rooms had ceilings of . . . ivory, the panels of which could slide back and let a rain of flowers, or of perfume from hidden sprinklers, shower upon his guests. . . . When the palace had been decorated throughout in this lavish style, Nero dedicated it, and condescended to remark, "Good, now I can at last begin to live like a human being!"

the old Rome and build a new one named after himself (Neropolis). Many felt their suspicions were confirmed when the emperor set aside a large tract of land that the fire had cleared in the heart of the city and built on it a new palace and pleasure park for his own use. It became known as the Golden House. When it was completed, Nero was reported to have said, "Good, now I can at last begin to live like a human being!" [62]

The creation of the Golden House only proves that Nero was self-centered and overly extravagant, however. The surviving evidence does not support the notion that he deliberately started the fire. To begin with, eyewitnesses saw the emperor rushing around the city, leading fire-fighting and relief efforts practically day and night for the six days the fire raged. Why would he risk life and limb if he wanted to see the city destroyed? Also, Nero was a selfish spendthrift. Burning down the whole city would only force him to waste huge sums on rebuilding projects, money he would rather spend on himself. Moreover, even the idea that he planned to burn just enough of the city to make way for the Golden House makes no sense. As Holland points out, "The area that he took over to build his new palace was far from the spot the blaze actually began." [63]

Another slanderous charge against Nero was that he unjustly blamed the fire on the Christians then living in Rome, using them as scapegoats to divert suspicion from himself. Tacitus claims:

Nero fabricated scapegoats, and punished with every refinement the notoriously depraved Christians. . . . Their originator, Christus [Jesus of Nazareth], had been executed in Tiberius's reign by the governor of [the province of] Judaea. . . . First, Nero had self-acknowledged Christians arrested. Then, on their information, large numbers of others were condemned, not so much for their [arson] as because the human race detested them. . . . Despite their guilt as Christians . . . the victims were pitied. For it was felt that they were being sacrificed to one man's brutality rather than to the national interest.[64]

The supposition that the Christians were unjustly persecuted in this instance assumes that they had nothing to do with the fire, or at least that no one had any credible reason to suspect them of foul play.

However, historians have begun reexamining these assumptions in recent years.

A seventeenth-century painting portrays the death of Seneca, the noted philosopher, whom Nero ordered to commit suicide.

First, it is possible that some Christians did help spread the fire once it had started by natural means. At the time, many of them believed that Jesus Christ would return imminently to destroy the old, corrupt world and establish his kingdom. Perhaps a few overly zealous individuals saw the city erupting in flames, believed the divine cleansing had begun, and thought it their duty to help it along. Even if only a handful were involved, it would have been enough to condemn all the rest. This is because the Christians, as Tacitus makes clear, were already suspected of depraved and criminal activities. Rumors spread that they killed babies and drank their blood in secret ceremonies, for example. Also, in Roman eyes, they worshiped a dead criminal. Thus, Nero's condemnation of the Christians may have been based on suspicions that seemed logical and real at the time. The trouble was that many people suspected *him* more than they did the Christians, hence the perception that Nero was making them scapegoats.

End of an Ignoble Reign

Whatever Nero's real motivations and role in the great fire and its aftermath might have been, many Romans continued to believe the worst about him. Not surprisingly, more than one assassination plot developed. The biggest, in 65, which involved several senators and even some members of the Praetorian Guard, was uncovered, and hundreds of people were tortured, executed, or banished. Among the dead was Seneca (who was forced to commit suicide).

After that, distrust and hatred for Nero were worse than ever. In March 68, several provincial governors and military generals rebelled and/or were acclaimed emperor by their troops. Soon the Senate and Praetorian Guard recognized the authority of one of these men, Servius Galba. Finally, Nero awoke one night in June to find his bodyguards gone and decided to flee. He hid in a villa a few miles north of the city until some soldiers found him, at which point, aided by a servant, he stabbed himself in the throat.

Thus ended the ignoble reign of the last ruler of the Julio-Claudian family, a man then only thirty-one. He might have lasted much longer with his mother at his side, for she had been far smarter, craftier, and more politically astute. But Nero had unwisely silenced Agrippina in her prime, and now he paid the price by joining her in oblivion.

Pliny the Elder and Galen: The Pursuit of Knowledge

T he Roman world produced a number of important thinkers and scholars who passed on their knowledge of the natural sciences in voluminous treatises. Of those whose works have survived, the two leading examples are Pliny the Elder and Galen. Pliny, who lived in the first century A.D., was an upper-class Roman whose huge *Natural History* covers such diverse subjects as astronomy, geography, botany, medicine, minerals and metals, and art and architecture. Galen was a second-century Greek physician who became the foremost medical practitioner and researcher in Rome. Their writings profoundly influenced later generations of Romans, not to mention the thinkers and writers of medieval and early modern times. (In fact, educated medieval

Europeans mistakenly concluded that Pliny and Galen, along with a handful of other Greco-Roman writers, were great, even infallible sages.)

Pliny and Galen were very different kinds of scholars. And a comparison of their methods and results illuminates the two major approaches to the pursuit of knowledge in the Roman world. The approach of Pliny and others like him, which was by far the more common, was to compile facts from existing manuscripts. (Most of these sources were by Greeks, often long-dead ones.) The result was usually a general overview that offered little or no new information derived from recent research. (If the overview covered a single subject, it was a handbook. If it covered many, as Pliny's did, it was an encyclopedia.) Fully aware of the lack of original research in his own time, Pliny wrote:

> In these glad times of peace, under an emperor [Titus] who so delights in the advancement of letters and science, no addition whatever is being made to knowledge by means of original research, and in fact even the discoveries of our predecessors are not being thoroughly studied. [65]

Apparently, Pliny did not see himself as part of the problem. Though he complained that little or no new research was being done, he personally lacked both the interest and training for such work. In his mind, there was plenty of room in scholarly circles for both compilers like himself and experimenters.

In marked contrast, Galen was one of the few scholars in the Roman period who uncovered new facts and ideas through his own experimentation. He was well aware that Roman doctors had created a broad-based medical institution and were often very efficient and effective healers. Yet he also noted that almost all of their knowledge was

Why Rome Had Little Use for Science

It is not completely clear why the Romans developed no substantial theoretical or experimental science of their own. Probably one contributing factor was the popularity of Stoicism, a philosophical movement that taught that the universe is endowed with divine purpose or intelligence (*logos*). Furthermore, it was thought that fate predetermines people's lives and that they should learn to live in harmony with nature, rather than question and probe it. In such a worldview, experimental science was seen as practically useless.

Also, as a people the Romans were often uncomfortable around or distrustful of intellectuals. Mainly conquerors, rulers, administrators, and businessmen, the Romans were primarily interested in maintaining order and the efficiency of their empire. And they viewed the traditional Greek intellectual as a clever but fairly useless person dwelling in an ivory tower. To the average Roman, manly action was far superior to "idle" speculation.

Because educated Romans had little interest in or time for science, handbooks and encyclopedias, like Pliny's, provided them a fast and convenient way to absorb the major knowledge of the day without having to understand the theory behind the facts. So even the most astute Roman thinkers, including Cicero, Seneca, and Pliny, were content to get much of their learning from general handbooks, many of which rehashed facts from previous handbooks.

based on long-established medical lore. As a dedicated doctor, it disturbed him that the better Roman physicians did no new research of their own and made no significant medical advances. Galen went much further in his own work. He dissected various animals, for instance. He then recorded what he learned from his research in a large body of writings, more than eighty of which have survived. They reveal a mind not content with the status quo but always striving to

Galen, the Greek doctor who became Rome's most renowned healer.

unlock knowledge still hidden from humanity.

Pliny's Education and Public Service

This is not to say that Pliny's intellect and love of knowledge was inferior to Galen's. Indeed, Pliny was a polymath (person of great and varied knowledge) of the first order, undoubtedly one of the most curious and educated men of the ancient world. What made the two men different was that Pliny's approach to knowledge was deeply rooted in the worldview of the Roman upper classes into which he was born.

Pliny was born in A.D. 23 in Novum Comum, a town in northern Italy. Gaius Plinius Secundus, who became known simply as Pliny, hailed from a wealthy family of the equestrian order. The equestrians (or knights) made up a Roman social class second in prestige only to the aristocratic patricians. To join the equestrians, a man (in this case Pliny's father or grandfather) had to be free, at least eighteen years old, of good moral character, and own property worth a minimum of 400,000 sesterces, a small fortune in ancient Rome. Pliny was extremely proud of this heritage. In his *Natural History,* he devotes a lengthy section to the history of the equestrians, saying in part, "The title of 'knight,' formerly [in early republican times] conferred if one could provide a horse for war, is now awarded on the basis of wealth." [66]

Because his family was well-off, Pliny received a first-rate education. For his higher learning, he went to Rome, where, like most other upper-class young men, he studied rhetoric. Then, at the age of about twenty-three or twenty-four, he entered the army as a junior officer. Stationed in both Upper and Lower Germany (provinces lying west of the Rhine River), Pliny saw some action against a German tribe. In another military posting, he became friendly with a fellow officer named Titus, son of the general Vespasian, both of whom later occupied the imperial throne.

When he was not involved in active military campaigning, Pliny the soldier had a good deal of time on his hands. He began to occupy it by writing. His first work was a treatise on the use of the javelin as a cavalry weapon. He also produced a history of Rome's wars against the Germanic tribes.

Pliny's interest in writing remained strong after he returned to Rome in 59, at the age of about thirty-six. At first he professed a desire to practice law, but soon found himself sidetracked, penning a set of grammar books. For the rest of his life, even during extended periods of public service, he spent many hours each day arduously researching old books and writing his own.

Those periods of public service began in 69, when Vespasian became emperor following the brief civil war that erupted after Nero's suicide. Pliny's former connections with Vespasian and Titus now paid off handsomely. The new emperor appointed the writer to a succession of major administrative posts in the provinces. Serving in Gaul, Spain, and Africa, Pliny spent much of his spare time gathering information about the

A fanciful modern depiction of Pliny the Elder, one of Rome's greatest scholars.

local flora, fauna, and other lore, data he later incorporated into his great masterwork on the natural sciences.

Phenomenal Dedication and Industry

Pliny labored on that tome, the *Natural History,* all through the 70s. It is an enormous collection of facts and anecdotes covering a wide range of subjects, all intended as general reference material for everyday

Pliny Comments on Life After Death

Pliny the Elder did not hesitate to inject his personal opinions about morality and religion into his great work of natural history. Here, for example, he explains why he disagrees with the concept of human souls living on in an afterlife.

There seems some confusion concerning the spirits of the departed after burial. All men are in the same state from their last day forward as they were before their first day, and neither body nor mind has any more sensation after death than it had before birth. But wishful thinking prolongs itself into the future and falsely invents for itself a life that continues beyond death, sometimes by giving the soul immortality or a change of shape, sometimes by according feeling to those below, worshipping spirits and deifying one who has already ceased to be even a man. . . . If we consider the soul separately, of what is it formed? . . . Where is its power of thought? . . . What is its abode and how great is the crowd of souls or shadows from so many ages past? These imaginings are characteristic of childish gibberish and of mortal men greedy for everlasting life. Similar also is the vanity about preserving the bodies of men. . . . A plague on this mad idea that life is renewed by death!

readers rather than scholars. "We need works of reference, not books," Pliny states in the work's preface. "In the thirty-seven books of my *Natural History,* I have, therefore, included the material derived from reading 2,000 volumes." [67] This estimate is overly modest; the actual figure was closer to 4,000.

Although Pliny's encyclopedia covers diverse topics in considerable detail, it is by no means rambling or disorganized. He seems to have devised an efficient system for classifying and collating his piles of sources and facts. And even though he was rarely original, he did list his sources in a careful, forthright manner; among these were 473

writers, 146 of them Latin and 327 foreign (mostly Greek). Pliny was so scrupulous, in fact, that he readily admitted when he had not read an author's original work but had merely noted the man's name in the bibliography of a handbook he had used. Most of his sources actually lacked bibliographies, as their authors tried to take credit for work they did not do. Pliny abhorred this practice, calling it dishonest and unprofessional. "You will count it as proof of my professionalism," he writes,

the fact that I have prefaced these books with the names of my authorities. In my opinion, such acknowledgment of those who have contributed to one's success . . . abounds with honorable modesty. . . . Surely it is characteristic of a mean spirit . . . to prefer to be caught committing a theft rather than to repay a loan.[68]

Despite the fact that Pliny contributed little new material of his own and relied mainly on compiling the works of others, his achievement remains impressive. The number of books he read, absorbed, sum-

A tireless researcher, Pliny pores over the works of earlier naturalists.

marized, and correlated was immense. Moreover, to accomplish such a feat while maintaining a full-time day job requires nothing less than phenomenal dedication and industry. In fact, Pliny was a workaholic who saw sleep as his enemy. In a revealing passage, he admits:

> I pursue my research in odd hours, that is at night. . . . I reckon up the sleep I need consistent with keeping well [i.e., I get just enough sleep to maintain my health]. I am content with this reward alone, in that . . . I prolong my life by many hours. For assuredly, to live is to be awake![69]

Fortunately, a longer and more detailed tract describing Pliny's unusual work habits has survived. It was written by his equally famous nephew, Pliny the Younger, in a letter to an acquaintance. "You may wonder how such a busy man was able to complete so many volumes," the younger Pliny states, considering that

> his time was much taken up with the important offices he held and his friendship with the Emperors. But he combined a penetrating intellect with amazing powers of concentration and the capacity to manage with the minimum of sleep. . . . [He] would rise half-way through the night; in winter it would often be at midnight or an hour later, and two [A.M.] at the latest. Admittedly he fell asleep very easily, and would often doze and wake up again during his work. Before daybreak he would visit the emperor Vespasian . . . and then go

to attend his official duties. After something to eat . . . in summer when he was not too busy he would often lie in the sun, and a book was read aloud [to him by his secretary] while he made notes and extracts. He made extracts of everything he read, and always said that there was no book so bad that some good could not be got out of it. . . . A book was read aloud during the meal and he took rapid notes. . . . To such lengths did he carry his passion for saving time. . . . [In fact] he thought any time which was not devoted to work was wasted.[70]

Demise of a Great Scholar

The incredible dedication the elder Pliny showed to his work and the cause of knowledge eventually contributed to his own demise. In the late 70s, he was appointed to oversee shipbuilding, repairs, and administration for the Roman fleet stationed at Misenum, on the Bay of Naples. It was there that he witnessed the start of the great eruption of the nearby volcano Mt. Vesuvius on August 24, A.D. 79. (This was the famous disaster that buried the towns of Pompeii and Herculaneum, preserving much of their contents for posterity.)

Mount Vesuvius spews out smoke and ash during an eruption. Pliny died trying to study the huge eruption of A.D. 79.

"My uncle . . . saw at once that it [the eruption] was important enough for a closer inspection," the younger Pliny later wrote. "He ordered a boat to be made ready, telling me that I could come with him if I wished. I replied that I preferred to go on with my studies." The older man then hurried away, "steering his course straight for the danger zone. He was entirely fearless, describing each new movement and phase of the eruption to be noted down [by his secretary] exactly as he observed them." Meanwhile, the younger Pliny recorded,

> on Mt. Vesuvius broad sheets of fire and leaping flames blazed at several points. . . . My uncle tried to allay the fears of his companions . . . [who were] in darkness, blacker and denser than any ordinary night, which they relieved by lighting torches. . . . My uncle decided to go down to the shore and investigate on the spot the possibility of any escape by sea, but he found the waves still too wild and dangerous. A sheet was spread on the ground for him to lie down, and he repeatedly asked for cold water to drink. [71]

Finally, the ash and poisonous fumes became too much for the great scholar. Two days later, a search party found his body on an ash-covered beach. Having literally given his life for science, Pliny left behind his great work of natural history, which was published soon after his passing. It remains important for its preservation of information from many earlier books that have not survived.

Galen's Enlightened Hometown

Galen performed a similar service, as he collected and commented on the writings of leading doctors of the past. In particular, he kept alive the important medical tradition initiated by the fifth-century-B.C. Greek physician Hippocrates, now called the "Father of Medicine." (Hippocrates and his students made an effort to keep medical theory separate from religion. For example, they held that disease is not a punishment meted out by the gods but, rather, a natural phenomenon governed by natural laws.) What made Galen different from Pliny was that Galen actively expanded on his sources, thereby revealing new knowledge.

Galen's thirst for knowledge was in large degree a function of his upbringing, as both his hometown and his family encouraged his intellectual pursuits. Galen was born about A.D. 130 in the Greek city of Pergamum (on the western coast of Asia Minor). Known for its rich and diverse cultural life and enlightened political atmosphere, Pergamum had the world's second largest library (after the one in Alexandria, Egypt). It also featured a major shrine honoring Asclepius, the Greek god of healing, which attracted medical researchers and other scholars and pilgrims from across the Roman world.

As for Galen's family, it was well-to-do. His father, Nicon, made his living as an engineer but devoted much of his free time to studying philosophy, literature, and other diverse subjects. Nicon insisted that his son receive a sound, well-rounded education

The Greek god of healing, Asclepius, with his symbol, a staff entwined by a snake.

and generous, and this awoke in me feelings of warmth and love for [my father]. . . . These, then . . . were the precepts I took from my father; and I keep them to this day. I do not declare allegiance to any sect, rather subjecting them all to a thorough examination; and I remain calm in the face of all events that may befall me from day to day. . . . Under my father's training I developed . . . respect for truth alone. [72]

Because of his close relationship with his father, Galen was surely deeply disturbed when Nicon died in about 148. Less than a year before, Nicon had urged his son to go into medicine, and the youth had begun studying with a respected anatomist who resided in Pergamum. Now, with his father gone, and having no desire to live alone with his mother (whom he described as a bad-tempered nag), the eighteen-year-old Galen decided to continue his medical studies in the nearby city of Smyrna.

Rome's Leading Medical Authority

The brilliant young Galen quickly absorbed all he could in Smyrna. And in the next few years, he traveled around the eastern Mediterranean, trying to expand his ever-growing store of medical knowledge. After stays in Crete, Cyprus, Phoenicia, and Palestine, he reached Alexandria and availed himself of the large number of medical writings in that city's great library.

Finally, in about 157, Galen returned to Pergamum and began attending wounded gladiators. It was valuable experience for a

and hired the best available tutors. Galen later credited his father with making him both a lover of learning and a critical thinker:

> I had the great good fortune to have a father who was extremely slow to anger, as well as extremely just, decent,

young doctor. More importantly for Galen, it represented a legal way of studying people's insides, since at the time the law forbade the dissection of human bodies. At the same time, he began penning books on medicine, of which he would eventually produce hundreds.

After a four-year stay in Pergamum, Galen moved on to Rome, hoping that he could learn even more in the capital of the known world. He was disappointed, however, by the ignorance and laziness of many of the Roman doctors he met. "Hippocrates set great store by accurate knowledge of the body," he complained:

These doctors fail, in their studies, to learn [about] . . . each part of the body. . . . Do [today's doctors] lack the potential and sufficient eagerness in their preparation for the art? . . . It must be because of the bad upbringing current in our times, and because of the higher value accorded to wealth as opposed to virtue, that we no longer get anyone of the quality of . . . Hippocrates among our doctors. [73]

With such mediocre competition, Galen rapidly gained a stellar reputation, and many rich and influential Romans flocked to his private practice and lectures. Upper-class society began calling him the "Wonder Worker," and eventually the reigning emperor, Marcus Aurelius, took an interest in him. When Marcus Aurelius later left Rome to fight the Germans, he made Galen personal physician to his son, the future emperor Commodus. Thereafter, secure in his

position as Rome's leading medical authority, Galen treated not only Commodus (who was assassinated in 192) but also his three successors—Pertinax, Didius Julianus, and Septimius Severus. Unfortunately, the details of the great doctor's life during his last years are obscure. It appears that he continued to turn out medical treatises at a prodigious rate and died in about 200.

Galen pauses while walking to study the anatomy of a human skeleton he has found.

A Man Ahead of His Time

These and Galen's other writings show that his personal investigations of human anatomy and bodily processes were revolutionary and far more advanced than the traditional medical knowledge of his day. Galen regularly dissected apes, dogs, pigs, and other animals and took detailed notes of what he saw. He studied the brain and nerves, purposely severing the spinal cord in various places and observing how this impaired the use of muscles and limbs. From this, he recognized that the brain directed bodily movements and was also the center of thought and reasoning. Galen was also the first medical researcher to suggest that the arteries contain blood, not air, as was previously thought (although he did not thoroughly understand the circulatory system). In addition, he made significant advances in examining the pulse and urine to diagnose illness.

Motivating Galen in these and his other researches was his unique attitude toward his work. He believed that his duty was not simply to heal but to advance the course

Galen Condemns the Abuse of Slaves

In addition to their value as documents in the history of medicine, Galen's writings supply important information about the lives of lower-class Romans of his time. This passage, for example, from his Affections and Errors of the Soul *(in P.N. Singer's selection of his works), documents the fairly common abuse of servants and slaves.*

Never did I lay hand upon a servant—a discipline practiced by my father too, who frequently berated friends who had bruised their hands in the act of hitting servants in the teeth. He would say that they [the masters] deserved to suffer convulsions and die from the inflammations they had sustained. . . . Once I even saw a man lose his temper and strike his servant in the eye with a reed-pen. And it is related of the emperor Hadrian [reigned 117–138] that he once struck one of his household staff in the eye with a pencil, causing him to lose the sight of one eye. When Hadrian realized what had happened, he summoned the servant and agreed to grant him a gift of his own request in exchange for the loss he had suffered. But the injured party was silent. Hadrian repeated his offer: that he [the servant] should request anything he wished. At which the servant grew bold and said that he wanted nothing but his eye back. For what gift could compensate for the loss of an eye?

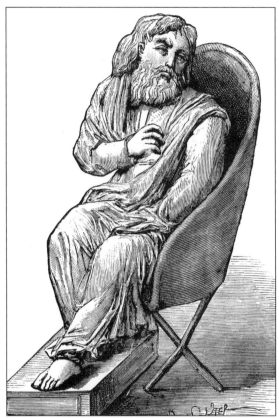

Galen in old age. Fortunately for later ages, many of his works have survived.

of human knowledge as well. In his work titled *The Best Doctor Is Also a Philosopher,* he stated,

The fact that we were born later than the ancients, and have inherited from them arts which they developed to such a high degree, should have been a considerable advantage. It would be easy, for example, to learn thoroughly in a very few years what Hippocrates discovered over a very long period of time, and then to devote the rest of one's life to the discovery of what remains. . . . There is nothing to prevent us, not only from reaching a similar attainment, but even from becoming better than him. For it is open to us to learn everything which he gave us a good account of, and then to find out the rest for ourselves.[74]

If Pliny and Rome's many other brilliant and talented scholars had held this same view, the Empire may well have gone on to produce an industrial and technological society; if so, it would easily have conquered the northern barbarians and never fallen. Clearly, then, Pliny was a product of his time, while Galen was ahead of his own. Had the reverse been true, history might have been very different.

Chapter 6

Hadrian and Antoninus: The Good Emperors

Edward Gibbon's famous eighteenth-century judgment that the combined reigns of the "five good emperors" (Nerva, Trajan, Hadrian, Antoninus Pius, and Marcus Aurelius) brought Rome its greatest era of peace and prosperity still rings true. It was, Gibbon adds, "possibly the only period of history in which the happiness of a great people was the sole object of government."[75] This last statement is something of an exaggeration when applied to all five of these rulers. However, it comes much closer to truth in the cases of Hadrian (reigned 117–138) and Antoninus (138–161), two of the most caring, constructive, and beneficent of all the Roman emperors. In Gibbon's words, they tried to show the peoples of the known world that Rome's immense power was motivated not simply by a desire for conquest but

> by the love of order and justice. During a long period of forty-three years, their virtuous labors were crowned with success; and if we except a few slight hostilities that served to exercise the legions of the frontier, the reigns of Hadrian and Antoninus Pius offer the fair prospect of universal peace. The Roman name was revered among the most remote nations of the earth.[76]

These two rulers had their faults, to be sure. Hadrian could be egotistical, personally distant, and overly suspicious of others, for example, and Antoninus lacked ambition and creativity. Yet these flaws pale in comparison with the extraordinary degree of efficiency, compassion, generosity, justice, and dedication to duty displayed by both men. On their watch, the Roman realm reached its height of security, affluence, and general welfare, a level it would never attain again.

The "Greekling"

Rome was already climbing toward that level when Hadrian, whose full name was Publius Aelius Hadrianus, was born in Rome in January 76. Vespasian was emperor then. In the wake of Nero's misrule and the short civil war that followed it, Vespasian, an honest and just ruler, was trying hard to reinstate good and constructive government.

It was this positive social and cultural atmosphere that nurtured the young Hadrian. His family, which had originated in northern Italy and resided for some time in Spain, was well-to-do and moved in influential circles. This proved fortunate for Hadrian sooner rather than later. When he was only ten, his father, Publius Aelius Hadrianus Afer, died, and the boy became the ward of two prominent men. The first was a well-to-do equestrian named Acilius Attianus; the other was Trajan, the future emperor, whose aunt, Ulpia, had married Hadrian's grandfather (which made Trajan and Hadrian second cousins).

Thanks to his new mentors, the young Hadrian prospered and received a good education. He was particularly fascinated by

The Affair of the Four Consuls

Although Hadrian was a just man and benign ruler, his reign began with a period of bad feelings between himself and the Senate. In this excerpt from his Chronicle of the Roman Emperors, *noted scholar Chris Scarre explains how the senators blamed the new emperor for the deaths of four of their number.*

These were all ex-consuls, men of the highest rank, and the incident is known as the "affair of the four consuls." The pretext for their deaths was that they were plotting his [Hadrian's] overthrow; [the Roman historian] Dio [Cassius], for one, did not believe this, and gave their wealth and influence as the real reason. What made the whole business particularly unattractive was Hadrian's refusal to accept any responsibility for these executions. . . . [He] declared that the deaths had been ordered by the Senate without his approval. Nevertheless, the matter remained so much in doubt that he swore a public oath that he was not the responsible party. He also wrote to the Senate promising not to put any senators to death without proper trial.

Greece and all things Greek, so much so that he soon earned the nickname *Graeculus*, or "Greekling." Later, in the 90s, Trajan's influence was also instrumental in securing for Hadrian, now a young man, a commission in the army. In the rank of tribune (one of six junior officers who helped administer each Roman legion), Hadrian served in Upper Germany and Pannonia (lying along the Danube River, northeast of Italy).

The political and military events of the years that followed continued to work in

Hadrian's wife, Vibia Sabina, appears in a likeness inspired by her images on coins.

Hadrian's favor. In 97, the emperor Nerva adopted Trajan, then governor of Upper Germany, as his heir, and only a few months later, in January 98, Nerva died unexpectedly. The young Hadrian carried the news to his cousin and was the first to congratulate him on his accession to the throne. Several months later Hadrian accompanied Trajan to Rome, where the new emperor received a warm welcome from the Senate and people. The bond between the two men now grew stronger than ever. In 100, Hadrian married Trajan's niece, Vibia Sabina. The emperor was also instrumental in helping Hadrian become governor of Pannonia in 107 and consul in 108.

An Imposing, Compassionate Ruler

In 114, Trajan appointed Hadrian to yet another important office—the governorship of Syria, one of Rome's eastern provinces. Hadrian was at this post when, in August 117, news arrived that Trajan had died in southern Asia Minor. The exact way that Hadrian succeeded his illustrious cousin is somewhat mysterious. Not long after the emperor's passing, his wife, Pompeia Plotina, announced that Trajan had formally adopted Hadrian a few days before his death. Although this may well have happened, the suspicion remains that the empress, who strongly favored Hadrian, forged the paperwork.

Whatever the true circumstances of the adoption, Hadrian, now forty-one, was emperor of the strongest realm on earth. And he rapidly made a positive impression on

The Boy Who Became a God

Hadrian had a young Greek friend named Antinous, who was rumored to be the emperor's lover. When Antinous died in a tragic drowning accident, Hadrian pronounced him a god and built temples and statues in his memory, as described in these memorable passages from the late scholar Royston Lambert's book about the two men, Beloved of God.

One day in the slanting sunlight of late October in the year A.D. 130, a body was found in the murky receding floodwaters of the river Nile. It was that of a young man, aged between eighteen and twenty, athletic in build, with . . . such unusual and poignant beauty that it was to haunt the imagination . . . of civilized men for nearly two thousand years. . . . His name . . . was Antinous. And he was a Greek boy, the beloved, if nothing more, of the fifty-four-year-old ruler of the Roman Empire, Hadrian. . . . Four years after drowning in the Nile, a cult of Antinous had extended throughout the Mediterranean world and penetrated to the very frontiers of the Empire. The earliest Christian commentators sneered that it had been forced on people by . . . Hadrian, and there can be no doubt that he had ardently promoted its spread. But in the . . . religious climate of the 130s, particularly in the Greek-speaking world, the advent of the god Antinous was greeted with a spontaneous enthusiasm which must have surprised even the emperor himself. . . . Meanwhile, the sculptors of Greece, Asia Minor, Italy, and Egypt had been hard at work creating . . . images of the new god-hero in marble or bronze. . . . Perhaps never in antiquity had so many . . . images been produced of one individual in so short a time, for most of them were made before Hadrian died in 138. A recent authority has calculated that . . . about 2,000 sculptures were produced in these eight years.

most of his subjects. His physical appearance was imposing, as described by modern biographer Royston Lambert:

Hadrian was fair-skinned, taller than average and of stalwart build. . . . He took great care about his external appearance, wearing the toga in Italy, an elegant, informal traveling outfit on his journeys, and Greek dress for the festivals of Athens. His hair was carefully combed forward in waves . . . and fell over his brow in dainty little curls. . . . He sported a short, well-barbered beard—the first emperor to do so—and all his successors were to follow suit.[77]

As for Hadrian's personal traits and qualities, he was noted for his courage and endurance as well as his keen intelligence. His memory was supposedly so good that he recalled the names of large numbers of soldiers whom he had met or seen only once; calling them by name when meeting them again years later gained him much respect in the ranks. He also earned the allegiance of his troops by visiting them in their camps, sitting and talking for long periods with the sick and wounded, and marching on foot along with the soldiers when they were on the move. (By custom, commanders rode on horses or in wagons.)

Hadrian also showed unusual compassion for ordinary citizens, including the poor and downtrodden, as revealed in some of his domestic policies. He expanded a program begun by Trajan that fed and clothed the poor, especially children. He also passed laws improving the lot of slaves. Among these was one that prohibited a master from killing a slave and another that banned the common practice of torturing all the slaves in a household when only one had killed the master.

Hadrian's Military Policies

In the international and military sphere, Hadrian largely reversed the policy of his predecessor, Trajan, who had embarked on several large military campaigns and expanded the size of the realm. In particular, Trajan had crossed the Euphrates River and overrun large parts of Mesopotamia and Armenia. Hadrian felt that the Empire was already big enough before these conquests; in fact, in his view it had become too big to administer and defend successfully on a long-term basis. So he pulled Roman forces back to Euphrates, abandoning the recently taken lands.

Hadrian concentrated instead on strengthening the Empire's existing borders in an effort to increase the security of the lands

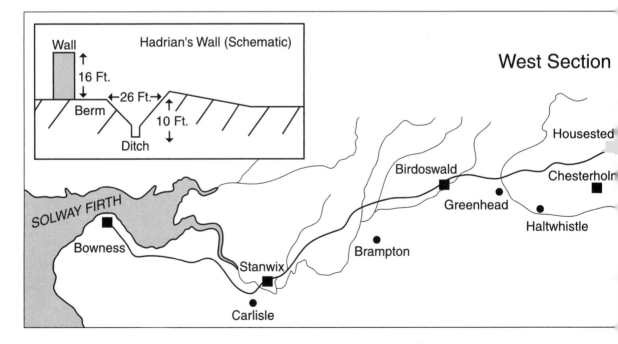

Rome had ruled for generations. He significantly reinforced and expanded the realm's northern defenses, which kept the Germanic and other "barbarian" tribes at bay. These defenses, consisting of wooden palisades backed up by forts at intervals, stretched for some twenty-five hundred miles, from the North Sea in the northwest to the Black Sea in the east.

Even more impressive was the defensive wall Hadrian began in 122 in Britain to protect the island's Roman-controlled lands from the Scottish tribes in the north. Hadrian's Wall, as it came to be known, was constructed of stone. It stood sixteen feet high, featured a moat twenty-six feet wide and ten feet deep, and stretched for some seventy-three miles. Supporting these defenses were 80 small castlelike forts spaced about a mile apart and 160 defensive towers. Hadrian's Wall was so extensive and well constructed that large portions of it are still intact.

A Great Traveler and Builder

The emperor was motivated to build the wall partly because he visited Britain in person and witnessed the vulnerability of the local Roman towns and farms. Indeed, travel became one of the great hallmarks of his reign. Hadrian traveled more extensively than any other Roman ruler, visiting nearly every province. In fact, he spent more time away from Rome than in it.

One crucial advantage of these extensive travels was that, as in the case of the wall in Britain, Hadrian saw for himself the needs of his subjects and their cities. As a result, he made more of an emotional investment

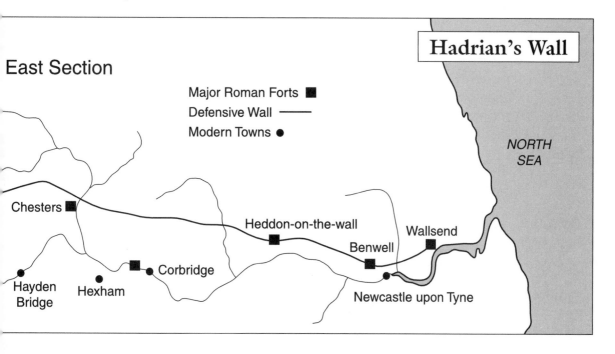

81

in them than most other emperors, who merely read about provincial needs in letters and petitions. Just as important, Hadrian's subjects, including soldiers in distant outposts and foreign rulers under Rome's control, saw him in the flesh, spoke with him, and felt connected. The overall result was a sound relationship between ruler and ruled and measurable improvements in the Empire's infrastructure and standard of living. Lambert elaborates:

> Wherever [Hadrian] went, frontiers were studied, defenses improved, roads built, legions exercised, client kings and vassals impressed and kept loyal. The cities through which he passed found themselves equipped with new harbors, markets, aqueducts, revised laws, with gymnasia and libraries, games and festivals, stadiums and theaters. Many new cities bearing his name rose from the virgin soil [including Hadrianopolis, later called Adrianople, in northern Greece]. The cults and temples of the gods . . . which he never failed to examine and to venerate, flourished again, adorned with magnificent buildings, sculptures and dedications. . . . Even now, after almost two thousand years, it is impossible not to be amazed at the extent and diversity of Hadrian's benefactions, at the inexhaustibility of his activity and at the speed and comprehensiveness of his travels. [78]

Among the most extensive of Hadrian's provincial building projects were those in Greece. This is hardly surprising considering how much he adored Greek culture. The emperor completed the Temple of Olympian Zeus in Athens, a structure the Athenians had begun centuries before but never finished. He also restored or erected various buildings at Olympia, site of the famous athletic games, and Delphi, home of the most respected oracle in the known world. (An oracle was a priestess who transmitted the words of a god to humans; her message and the shrine she inhabited were also referred to as oracles.)

Hadrian's builders and artisans did not neglect Rome and Italy. In the capital, he had them rebuild the Pantheon, a huge domed structure first erected by Augustus's friend and son-in-law, Marcus Agrippa. And in the countryside near Tivoli, about eighteen miles northeast of Rome, rose Hadrian's villa. The largest personal residence in the world at the time, it consisted of a palace and several long roofed walkways, gardens, and bathhouses. Hadrian also installed numerous small-scale replicas of buildings he had seen and admired during his travels throughout the Mediterranean.

The Succession

Hadrian was able to accomplish so many vigorous travels and large-scale projects partly because he long remained a vital, hardy individual. In 136, however, having reached his sixtieth year, he was beset by illness. (It may have been a form of edema, excessive fluid buildup in the tissues.) Worried about the succession, that year the emperor adopted as his heir a respected senator named Lucius Ceionius Commodus. However,

A reconstruction of Hadrian's villa at Tivoli. The complex contained reproductions of buildings from across the known world.

Commodus died of tuberculosis in early January 138.

Growing increasingly sick and weak, Hadrian realized that he had to choose another heir. This time he picked his closest political adviser, Antoninus, who was formally adopted in February 138. The emperor wanted the succession to be as secure and smooth as possible and planned for the contingency that Antoninus, who was already fifty-one, might die in the near future. Accordingly, at the same time that Hadrian adopted Antoninus, the latter adopted Marcus Annius Verus (later known as Marcus Aurelius).

Hadrian had put his affairs in order none too soon. On July 10, 138, he finally succumbed to his illness. According to an ancient biographer, while on his deathbed the emperor, who fancied himself a poet, composed these enigmatic lines:

> Little charmer, wanderer, little sprite,
> Body's companion and guest,
> To what places now will you take
>   flight,
> Forbidding and empty and dim as
>   night?[79]

Antoninus's Rise to Power

Hadrian died at Baiae, a small town on the northern rim of the Bay of Naples. Antoninus was in Rome when the news reached him that he was the new emperor. Considering

Hadrian Adopts Antoninus

According to Dio Cassius (in a summary of his history compiled by the Byzantine writer Xiphilinus), Hadrian made the following speech to the Roman notables who had gathered to witness Antoninus's official adoption as the emperor's heir.

I, my friends, have not been permitted by nature to have a son, but you have made it possible by legal enactment. . . . The man whom I now give you [is] one who is noble, mild, tractable, and prudent, neither young enough to do anything reckless, nor so old as to neglect anything, one who has been brought up according to the laws and one who has exercised authority in accordance with our traditions, so that he is not ignorant of any matters pertaining to the imperial office, but can handle them all effectively. I refer to Aurelius Antoninus here. Although I know him to be the least inclined of men to become involved in affairs [of state] and to be far from desiring any such power, still I think that he will not deliberately disregard either me or you, but will accept the office even against his will.

the enormity of the office, it is quite probable that he took a moment to reflect back on how the events of his life had brought him to this fateful and sobering moment. He was born Titus Aurelius Fulvus Boionius Antoninus on September 19, 86, during the reign of Vespasian's son, Domitian. The birth took place at Lanuvium, a town on the plain of Latium, about twenty miles south of Rome; however, Antoninus spent most of his boyhood at the family's estate at Lorium, ten miles west of the capital. (Later, as emperor, he would build a small palace in Lorium.)

Antoninus was still very young when his father, Titus Aurelius Fulvus, who had been consul in 89, died. Following custom, the boy entered the home and guardianship of the closest living paterfamilias (father figure) in the family, his father's father. Later, Antoninus was raised by his other grandfather, Arrius Antoninus. It was from this maternal grandfather that the young man took the name Antoninus. (It was then common among upper-class Romans to adopt names from men in the family's female line.)

In about 110, when he was twenty-four, Antoninus married sixteen-year-old Annia Galeria Faustina (or Faustina the Elder), the daughter of a prominent provincial nobleman. It seems certain that the couple enjoyed a genuinely affectionate relationship. She supported him in his climb up the standard ladder of political offices (quaestor, praetor, and finally consul in 120), and she traveled with him to the province of Asia (in western Asia Minor) when he became its governor in the mid-130s. Antoninus is credited with this remark about his wife: "By heaven I would rather live with her on Gyara [a bleak Aegean island where people were often exiled] than in the palace without her." [80]

Unfortunately for Antoninus, the last part of this statement came to pass, as Faustina died in the third year of his reign. The grief-stricken emperor erected a temple to her, a beautiful structure that still stands in Rome; he also dedicated a new charity to her, one that provided aid to

homeless girls, and set up gold and silver statues in her memory. This was not the only family tragedy Antoninus had to endure. Three of the four children he had had with Faustina—two boys and two girls—died young. Only Faustina the Younger survived.

Antoninus (right) and his wife, Faustina. She died young, as did three of their four children.

(She married Marcus Aurelius, helping to ensure the dynastic succession.)

"He Was Praiseworthy in Every Respect"

The public welfare program the emperor set up in his departed wife's name was only one of many he supported. He maintained or expanded those that Trajan and Hadrian had instituted, including relief for the poor, widows and orphans, and other underprivileged groups. He also followed Hadrian's lead in passing more enlightened legislation regarding slaves. Under Antoninus, a master who killed a slave without just cause was liable to the same punishment he would receive for killing another master's slave. (This may not seem all that enlightened today, when the mere existence of slavery is widely viewed as unacceptable; however, it must be remembered that at the time, the institution was so entrenched and taken for granted that no one, including the Christians or even the slaves themselves, seriously considered the idea of abolishing it.)

These policies are only part of the evidence for Antoninus's unusually caring and compassionate nature. Not long after he ascended the throne, the Senate conferred on him the added name of Pius, or "dutiful." A later ancient source claims that he earned this honor by keeping Hadrian from committing suicide during his painful last months of life, and "because he was in fact most merciful by nature and did no harsh deed in his own times."[81] Noted historian Michael Grant adds other likely reasons for the honor, namely "Antoninus's meticu-

lousness [strict attention to detail] in matters of religion . . . and his graciousness of character and correct performance of all of his duties, in every branch of life, relating both to gods and to humankind."[82]

Indeed, the ancient sources are unanimous in praising Antoninus's character. According to one writer:

> His natural capacities were brilliant and his character kindly. . . . [He was] a man of moderation, and a thrifty landowner, of mild disposition. . . . He was generous and he kept away from what belonged to others. All these qualities were in balance and without ostentation [showiness]. In short, he was praiseworthy in every respect.[83]

The most detailed and revealing contemporary portrait of Antoninus comes from someone who knew him intimately—his adopted son, Marcus Aurelius. "In my father I observed mildness of temper, and unchangeable resolution in the things which he had determined [to do]," Aurelius begins,

> and no vainglory [conceit] in those things which men call honors; and a love of labor and perseverance; and a readiness to listen to [others] . . . and to be satisfied on all occasions, and cheerful . . . and to be ever watchful over the things which are necessary for the administration of the Empire, and to be a good manager of the [state budget]. . . . He showed sobriety in all things and firmness, and never any mean thoughts or action. . . . There

Marcus Aurelius, Antoninus's adopted son and Rome's sixteenth emperor.

was in him nothing harsh nor implacable, nor violent . . . but [instead] he examined all things . . . as if he had an abundance of time, and without confusion, in an orderly way, vigorously and consistently.[84]

Rome's Shining Moment

These passages make Antoninus sound like a veritable saint whose reign was unblemished by any sort of injustice, unrest, or violence. The reality was that in a realm as large and diverse as the Roman Empire, unrest was bound to exist from time to time; Antoninus's reign was no exception. In 140,

in Britain, a local tribe rebelled and Antoninus ordered one of his generals, Quintus Lollius Urbicus, to quell the uprising. Urbicus also expanded Roman territory northward, beyond Hadrian's Wall. This campaign culminated in the erection of a new defensive fortification running east to west across northern Britain—the Antonine Wall. Antoninus's armies also put down local rebellions or fought bands of brigands in Africa, Greece, and Egypt.

Still, when compared to the troubles and military campaigns during the reigns of most other emperors, those of Antoninus seem minor. Under his watch, Grant points out, such events "took place far from the principal centers of the Empire and their inhabitants, and . . . enabled force to be kept . . . away from them so they could live out their peaceful lives."[85] It was no wonder, then, that writers of many nationalities heaped praises on the realm during its zenith—the years that Hadrian and Antoninus ruled it. In the most famous of the surviving panegyrics (formal speeches of praise), composed partway through Antoninus's reign, a Greek named Aelius Aristides exclaimed,

> Every place is full of gymnasia, fountains, gateways, temples, shops, and schools! . . . Gifts never stop flowing from you [the Romans] to the cities . . . [which] shine in radiance and beauty. . . . Only those outside your Empire, if there are any, are fit to be pitied for losing such blessings. . . . Greek and [non-Greek] can now readily go [in

This nineteenth-century painting reflects the romantic vision of Rome expressed by Aelius Aristides in his great hymn of praise.

safety] wherever they please with their property or without it. . . . You have surveyed the whole world, built bridges of all sorts across rivers, cut down mountains to make paths for chariots,

filled the deserts with hostels, and civilized it all with system and order.[86]

Indeed, when Antoninus died peacefully of natural causes at age eighty-five in March 161, Roman law and order, prosperity, military power, and civilized culture appeared invincible, inevitable, perhaps even eternal. However, one of the great lessons of history is that nothing, no matter how good (or how bad), is permanent. Antoninus's successor, Marcus Aurelius, who was as good and well meaning as his adoptive father, would learn this lesson the hard way in a reign marred by plague and foreign invasions. And future generations of Romans, inhabiting a steadily declining realm, would look back at the reigns of Hadrian and Antoninus as their nation's shining moment in time's relentless march.

Chapter 7

Constantine and Ambrose: Christianizing the Empire

In the century following the reigns of Hadrian, Antoninus Pius, and Marcus Aurelius, the Roman Empire underwent several profound changes. In the mid–third century, a series of foreign invasions, economic setbacks, and civil conflicts brought the realm to the brink of collapse. Fortunately for Rome, a group of strong military leaders, foremost among them Diocletian (reigned 284–305), eventually restored order. But the new realm, today often referred to as the Later Empire, was a far less prosperous, secure, and happy place than the Rome of the Pax Romana.

It was during the Later Empire that the most significant change of all occurred: Christianity rapidly rose to the status of Rome's official religion. Christian leaders and ideas spread through and reshaped Roman culture in the Empire's final years; they also went on to exert powerful religious and political authority in the medieval and early modern ages that followed.

These events would likely not have occurred (or at least not in the same manner) had it not been for the intervention of two highly influential Romans. The first was the emperor Constantine I, known as Constantine the Great, who ruled from 306 to 337. He befriended the Christians when they were still a distrusted, persecuted group; granted them religious toleration and economic and other privileges; and eventually converted to the faith, lending it legitimacy and social acceptance. Later in that century, Ambrose, bishop of

Milan, helped to turn that new social acceptance into real political power. Ambrose strongly influenced the policies of a series of emperors. More than anyone else in his era, he was responsible for subordinating the government to the church and discouraging pagan worship.

Constantine and the Great Persecution

To appreciate what Constantine and Ambrose did for the Christian Church, one need only consider what life was like for Christians when Constantine was still a boy. Very little is known about his childhood. Even the year of his birth is uncertain, although 273, give or take a few years, seems

likely. Constantine was born Flavius Valerius Constantinus at Naissus, in the province of Upper Moesia (what is now Serbia). His father was Constantius I Chlorus, a noted military leader and close associate of Diocletian; Constantine's mother, Helena, with whom he had an exceptionally close relationship, began as a waitress in a bar and ended up a Christian saint (an honor accorded her after her death).

The connection Constantine's father had with Diocletian turned out to be fortunate for the family. In 284, Diocletian ascended the imperial throne and his chief lieutenants, including Constantius, became extremely powerful and privileged men. In 293, when Constantine was about twenty,

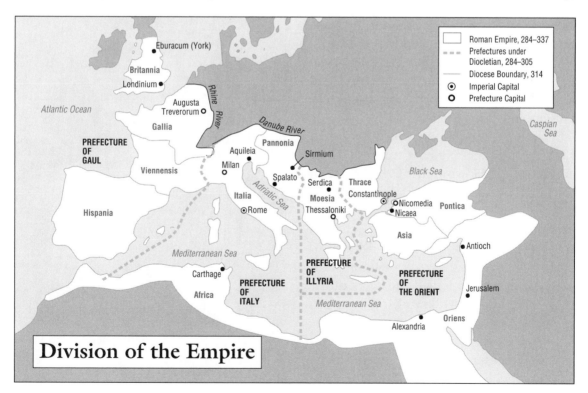

Division of the Empire

Diocletian appointed his father to a position in the Tetrarchy, a four-man team that ran the Empire for the next several years. (Diocletian remained the senior ruler of the group.) Constantius had control of Gaul and Britain and selected as his regional capital the city of Trier (in what is now northern France).

Sometime during these years, Constantine, and likely his whole family, must have developed a friendship, or at least a positive relationship, with some local Christians. It is otherwise difficult to explain why both father and son treated the Christians so humanely during the worst Christian persecution ever perpetrated by the Roman government. At the dawn of the fourth century, the Christians were still a relatively small minority in the Roman melting pot; they undoubtedly made up less than 10 percent of the population, and probably less than 5 percent. Moreover, they were still widely hated, mistrusted, and suspected of criminal behavior (killing babies, cannibalism, and so forth).

The great persecution, which the young Constantine personally witnessed, came about in the following manner. Diocletian tolerated the Christians at first, although he worried that the crimes attributed to them might anger the traditional gods and turn them against Rome. He finally decided to act in 303 following a traditional state religious ceremony in which the livers of the slaughtered animals did not look right to the priests. Someone suggested that some Christians had cast an evil spell. And the emperor's second in command, Galerius, who had a particular hatred of Christians, con-

vinced Diocletian to close the Christian churches. Soon, numerous Christian writings were burned and many members of the sect killed or jailed. The Christian bishop Eusebius later recalled seeing "the houses of prayer cast down to their foundations," and the prisons so filled up with Christians "that there was no longer any room left for real criminals." [87]

These terrible acts occurred almost exclusively in the eastern part of the realm, where Diocletian, Galerius, and their cronies held sway. In the west, by contrast, Constan-

This engraving of Diocletian is based on a surviving statue of the emperor.

tius showed the Christians mercy. He closed some churches, perhaps to make it look like he was following the party line, but took no further action. Moreover, when Constantine eventually succeeded his father, he treated the Christians in Gaul and Britain no differently than he did any other Roman citizens. This kindly treatment of the Christians would later have huge consequences for Constantine's career and the realm as a whole.

Tetrarchs, Usurpers, and Miracles

Meanwhile, as the great persecution continued in the east, political events began to conspire against the young Constantine, threatening to ruin his chances of rising to a position of power in the west. In 305, Diocletian, the senior emperor, suddenly abdicated the throne (an unprecedented act). He wanted the Tetrarchy to continue in force, but with a different combination of men. When he convened a meeting of soldiers and courtiers to announce his appointments, almost everyone present expected that Constantine would be named as his father's second-in-command in the west. "The gaze of all was upon Constantine," wrote the fourth-century Christian writer Lactantius:

No one had any doubt; the soldiers who were present, the military officers . . . had eyes only for him; they were delighted with him . . . they were making their prayers for him. . . . The old man [Diocletian] addressed them. . . . He was frail, he said, and was seeking

rest after his labors; so he was handing over the imperial power to men who were more robust. [88]

Diocletian did not choose Constantine, however. Instead, he appointed an army general named Severus to be Constantius's assistant emperor.

Constantine must have been sorely disappointed at being passed over for the Tetrarchy. But he was not about to let this setback keep him from remaining at his father's side. Crossing the English Channel into Britain, the young man joined Constantius in a military campaign against the Picts, a tribal people inhabiting what is now Scotland, who had been raiding Roman towns and farms. In the midst of this endeavor, in July 306, Constantius, who had been ill for some time, died. His troops happily proclaimed Constantine emperor in his place, so the ambitious young man became a member of the Tetrarchy after all.

However, that four-man ruling coalition was not fated to last much longer. In 307, less than a year after Constantius's death, a civil war erupted among the tetrarchs and several other powerful men intent on acquiring power for themselves. One of the usurpers, Maxentius, son of the retired tetrarch Maximian, seized the city of Rome. Maximian joined his son and then offered Constantine a chance to share power with them. Constantine accepted and married Maximian's daughter, Fausta, to seal the agreement.

The alliance fell apart, however, when Maximian quarreled with Maxentius. After much political infighting and betrayal, this

Maximian, one of the original tetrarchs and father of Maxentius.

new round of civil strife reached a dramatic conclusion in 312, as Constantine and Maxentius clashed outside the walls of Rome. According to Eusebius, the day before the battle, Constantine and his men observed a great shining cross in the sky; in addition, Christ came to Constantine in a dream and ordered him to use a Christian symbol as a battle emblem.

The truth of these miracles remains uncertain and debatable, since Eusebius, the only source for them, was an avid promoter of the Christian cause and therefore biased. Better documented is what happened the next day. Constantine ordered his soldiers to paint a Christian symbol onto their shields and attacked Maxentius at Rome's Milvian Bridge, where the latter suffered a decisive defeat and drowned in the Tiber River.

Constantine Repays the Christians

Constantine now felt indebted to the Christians and their deity for aiding in his great victory. He repaid them by granting them religious toleration, the biggest boost the faith had received since its founding. The official decree was known as the Edict of Milan. The name came from a meeting held in that city in February 313 between Constantine, now firmly in control of the western part of the realm, and Valerius Licinius, master of most of the eastern part. (While in Milan, the two men agreed on the content of the decree, and Licinius later issued it in both their names after returning to the east.) "[We] give both to Christians and to all others free facility to follow the religion which each may desire," the document stated.

> All restrictions which were previously put forward in official pronouncements concerning the sect of the Christians should be removed, and . . . each one of them who freely and sincerely carries out the purpose of observing the Christian religion may endeavor to practice its precepts without any fear or danger. [89]

(It is important to point out that neither Constantine nor Licinius had converted to

Christianity. In fact, Constantine long remained a pagan who accepted and showed favor to the Christian god along with a number of other traditional deities.)

In time, the good relations Constantine and Licinius had established at Milan deteriorated and the two clashed in still another civil war. The climax came at Adrianople, in northern Greece, on July 3, 324, with an overwhelming victory by Constantine. In the remaining thirteen years of his reign, he was the Empire's sole ruler, one of the last five emperors to control both the western and eastern Roman spheres. [90]

During these final years on the throne, Constantine continued to support the Christians, who made enormous social and political strides as a result. He granted Christian clergymen generous government subsidies, for example. The emperor also invited leading bishops to the imperial court, where they became a permanent fixture. In addition, Constantine mediated some serious disputes that arose among the bishops and brought them together in large-scale meetings to determine important matters of church doctrine. The most celebrated of these gatherings took place in 325 at Nicaea, in Asia Minor (the first of seven "Ecumenical Councils" held by the Christian Church over the course of the next four centuries).

"Conquer by This"

This excerpt from Eusebius's Life of Constantine *describes the supposed miracles that occurred just prior to the Battle of the Milvian Bridge in A.D. 312.*

While he [Constantine] was . . . praying with fervent entreaty, a most marvelous sign appeared to him from heaven. . . . He said that at about noon, when the day was already beginning to decline, he saw with his own eyes the trophy of a cross of light in the heavens, above the sun, and an inscription, CONQUER BY THIS, attached to it. At this sight he himself was struck with amazement, and his whole army also, which followed him on his expedition and witnessed the miracle. . . . And while he continued to ponder and reason on its meaning, night overtook him; then in his sleep the Christ of God appeared to him with the same sign which he had seen in the heavens, and commanded him to make a like of that sign . . . and to use it as a safeguard in all engagements with his enemies. . . . The emperor constantly made use of this sign of salvation as a safeguard against every adverse and hostile power, and commanded that others similar to it should be carried at the head of all his armies.

Another way Constantine benefited both Christianity and the realm was by establishing the city of Constantinople ("the city of Constantine") in 330 on the Bosporus Strait, on the southern rim of the Black Sea. He wanted to create a strong defensive point from which to protect the Empire's eastern flank. But the city was also conceived from the very beginning as a Christian stronghold, and Constantine and his successors erected numerous churches there.

Constantine wanted to do even more for the Christians. However, he fell ill shortly before Easter in 337 and died. While on his deathbed, he asked to be baptized a Christian; the bishop of Nicomedia (near Nicaea) performed the rite. That Constantine received this sacrament so late in life does not mean that he had harbored doubts about the faith. By the 330s he was a committed Christian, but as scholar Averil Cameron points out, at the time "baptism was taken very seriously and it was common to defer it as late as possible so that there was less chance of committing mortal sin subsequently."[91]

Ambrose's Early Years

In only a few short years, Constantine had laid the groundwork for a Christian revolution of enormous proportions and influence. His three sons (Constans, Constantine II, and Constantius II) were all devout Christians, as were all the Roman emperors who followed them except for one (Julian, who ruled from 361 to 363). In the increasingly pro-Christian social and political climate, paganism came under attack in many quarters. Some Christians grew bold and militant and vandalized or destroyed pagan statues, shrines, and temples across the realm. Zealous Christian priests denounced pagan beliefs and worship, and the bishops of the faith wielded more and more influence over the government.

Perhaps the most influential of all these bishops was Ambrose of Milan, who helped complete the Christian revolution that Constantine had started and became one of the great "doctors" (pivotal early leaders) of the western church. Ambrose was born in Trier, Constantius's and Constantine's

One of many Renaissance depictions of Constantine and his mother, Helena.

The Edict of Toleration

The following is part of the Edict of Milan (quoted in Tierney's The Middle Ages*), issued in 313, which granted religious toleration to the Christians and restored their confiscated property as well.*

We, Constantine and Licinius the Emperors, having met in concord in Milan . . . give both to Christians and to all others free facility to follow the religion which each may desire, so that by this means whatever divinity is enthroned in heaven may be gracious and favorable to us and to all who have been placed under our authority. . . . It is our pleasure that all restrictions which were previously put forward in official pronouncements concerning the sect of the Christians should be removed, and that each one of them who freely and sincerely carries out the purpose of observing the Christian religion may endeavor to practice its precepts without any fear or danger. . . . We have given free and absolute permission to practice their religion to the Christians. . . . We have decided furthermore to decree the following in respect of the Christians: if those places at which they were accustomed in former times to hold their meetings . . . [have been confiscated by the state], let the [state] be willing and swift to restore them to the Christians . . . without trying to ask a price.

home base, in about the year 340. It appears that the boy bore the same name as his father, Aurelius Ambrosius, who headed a well-to-do senatorial family. The family was Christian, although exactly when the elder Ambrosius converted to the faith is unknown. He served as governor of southern Gaul before dying when his son was still quite young.

The family then moved to Rome, where Ambrose and his brother, Satyrus, received first-class educations and headed down the path of traditional professional and government careers. In 365 Ambrose became a lawyer in Sirmium, in Pannonia, and in 370 he was appointed governor of Aemilia-Liguria, a small province in northern Italy with Milan as its chief city.

A Devout and Stubborn Man

It was during his fifth year of official residence in Milan that Ambrose's life abruptly took a turn down a decidedly unexpected path. The bishop of Milan died and Ambrose took part in a public meeting convened to discuss a replacement. To Ambrose's surprise, the crowd began to chant his name and demanded that he become the new bishop. At first he was extremely reluctant, as he had no solid foundation in theology; in fact, he was so against

This fifteenth-century painting shows Ambrose at work in his study.

the idea that he attempted to flee the city to escape his well-wishers. However, when the emperor, Gratian, expressed his desire that Ambrose take the job, Ambrose, out of a sense of duty, gave in. During a hectic marathon session lasting eight days, local clergymen ran the new initiate through the various religious ceremonies and posts one usually held before becoming a bishop.

Finally, Ambrose assumed a place among the church's elite.

To his credit, and despite his earlier reluctance, Ambrose took his new job very seriously. He was devout and quite conservative in his religious views, often taking the side of the poor and underprivileged against the rich and influential, as Jesus had. For instance, Ambrose insisted that his priests stop inviting so many well-to-do citizens to church-sponsored feasts and instead reach out to the poor, who were more in need of sustenance.

Ambrose could also be extremely stubborn and uncompromising when he thought he was right. In particular, he showed no tolerance or respect for the religious views of others. In his mind, Christianity was the only true religion and pagan beliefs must be suppressed and eradicated. Accordingly, he convinced Gratian to step down as chief priest of the state religion, a post all the emperors had traditionally held. Also at Ambrose's urging, Gratian confiscated the funds of the state priesthood and in 382 removed the time-honored statue of the goddess Victory from the Roman Senate.

Not surprisingly, the removal of the statue stirred up a storm of protest from leading non-Christians, who viewed the act as intolerant and insensitive. They eventually asked Quintus Aurelius Symmachus, a respected nobleman and senator, to plead their case to Gratian's co-emperor, Valentinian II. "The glory of these times makes it suitable that we defend the institutions of our ancestors and the rights and destiny of our country," Symmachus began.

We demand then the restoration of that condition of religious affairs which was so long advantageous to the state. . . . We beseech you, as old men, to leave to posterity what we received as boys. The love of custom is great. . . . We ask, then, for peace for the gods of our fathers and of our country. It is just that all worship should be considered as one. We look on the same stars, the sky is common [to all], the same world surrounds us. What difference does it make by what pains each seeks the truth? We cannot attain to so great a secret by one road. [92]

Ambrose delivers a sermon in this sixteenth-century painting, in which the artist depicts the bishop and his listeners in Renaissance garb.

Ambrose personally answered this plea, saying,

> [Symmachus] complains with sad and tearful words, asking . . . for the restoration of the rites of [the] ancient ceremonies. . . . Your sacrifice is a rite of being sprinkled with the blood of beasts. Why do you seek the voice of God in dead animals? . . . By one road, says he, one cannot attain to so great a secret. What you know not . . . we know by the voice of God. And what you seek by fancies, we have found out from the very Wisdom and Truth of God. Your ways, therefore, do not agree with ours. . . . You worship the works of your own hands; we think it an offense that anything which can be made should be esteemed God. God wills not that He should be worshipped in stones.[93]

Ambrose and Theodosius

Thanks to Ambrose, the statue was never returned to the Senate and the affair was widely viewed as a major victory of Christianity over paganism. The bishop of Milan was now the most powerful religious figure in the Roman world, and he continued to expand Christian influence in state affairs during the reign of Gratian and Valentinian's successor, Theodosius I. Though Theodosius was a devout Christian, Ambrose felt that he was too respectful of and soft on non-Christians.

This became clear during the first major clash between the two men. Some mil-itant Christians burned down a Jewish synagogue, and as part of the punishment Theodosius ordered the vandals to rebuild the structure. Incensed by this ruling, Ambrose stepped in and convinced the emperor that it would be unseemly for Christians to be forced to erect a Jewish building. So the synagogue remained in ruins and the perpetrators were never punished. As noted Christian scholar Justo Gonzalez puts it, "This was a sad precedent, for it meant that in an empire calling itself Christian, those whose faith was different would not be protected by the law."[94]

Ambrose's hold over Theodosius grew tighter as time went on. In 390, after a riot had destroyed part of the city of Thessaloniki (in northern Greece), the emperor ordered a stern punishment. The army herded more than seven thousand people into the local racetrack and mercilessly slaughtered them. Again displeased with Theodosius, Ambrose boldly rebuked him. When the emperor tried to attend church the following Sunday, the bishop stood in the doorway and denied him entrance; Ambrose also demanded that Theodosius repent his brutal act in public. No one had ever made such demands of a Roman emperor and lived, yet to the shock of many soldiers and courtiers, Theodosius gave in and repented.

After that, Theodosius acceded to nearly all of Ambrose's requests and demands. At the bishop's urging, the emperor banned all pagan sacrifices and cults and closed the pagan temples. (Some were destroyed, others

Ambrose Scolds the Emperor

Here is part of Ambrose's letter to Theodosius (quoted in Letters of St. Ambrose*) rebuking him for his slaughter of the former rioters at Thessaloniki.*

Listen, august Emperor. I cannot deny that you have a zeal for the faith; I do confess that you have the fear of God. But you have a natural vehemence [temper], which if anyone endeavors to soothe, you quickly turn to mercy; if anyone stirs you up, you rouse it so much more that you can scarcely restrain it. . . . There was done in the city of the Thessalonians [a terrible deed] of which no similar record exists, which I was not able to prevent happening. . . . I urge, I beg, I exhort, I warn, for it is a grief to me that you who were an example of unusual piety . . . should not mourn that so many have perished. . . . Conquer [the devil] while you still possess [the strength to do so]. Do not add another sin to your sin by a course of action that has injured many.

Ambrose stops Theodosius from entering church after the slaughter at Thessaloniki.

converted into museums, and still others remodeled as Christian churches.) The wholesale dismantling of the old religion was still ongoing when Ambrose died on Easter Sunday in April 397. He left behind a number of treatises on the Old Testament; one on the New Testament; several funeral orations and sermons; ninety-one letters; and, most important of all, the surety that his faith would have the strength and authority to outlast Rome and shape the future course of Western civilization.

Notes

Introduction: Talent, Energy, and Persistence Leave Their Mark

1. Sallust, *The Conspiracy of Catiline*, in *Sallust: The Jugurthine War/The Conspiracy of Catiline*, trans. S.A. Handford. New York: Penguin Books, 1988, p. 176.
2. Cicero, *On the State*, excerpted in *Cicero: On Government*, trans. Michael Grant. New York: Penguin Books, 1993, p. 189.
3. Edward Gibbon, *The Decline and Fall of the Roman Empire*, ed. David Womersley. 3 vols. New York: Penguin Books, 1994, vol. 1, p. 37.

Chapter 1: Virgil and Livy: Shapers of Rome's Proud Past

4. P.G. Walsh, *Livy: His Historical Aims and Methods*. New York: Cambridge University Press, 1967, pp. 10–11.
5. Aelius Donatus, *Life of Virgil*, trans. David Wilson-Okamura. 1996. http://virgil.org, p. 2.
6. Garry Wills, ed., *Roman Culture: Weapons and the Man*. New York: George Braziller, 1966, p. 24.
7. J. Wight Duff, *A Literary History of Rome, from the Origins to the Close of the Golden Age*. New York: Barnes and Noble, 1960, p. 329.
8. Donatus, *Life of Virgil*, pp. 3–4.
9. Virgil, *Eclogue* 1. 45. Translated by the author.
10. Virgil, *Georgic* 1. 498–503. Translated by the author.
11. Duff, *A Literary History of Rome*, p. 337.
12. Donatus, *Life of Virgil*, p. 6.
13. Walsh, *Livy*, pp. 1–2.
14. Livy, *The History of Rome from Its Foundation*, books 1–5 published as *Livy: The Early History of Rome*, trans. Aubrey de Sélincourt. New York: Penguin Books, 1960, p. 34.
15. Pliny the Younger, *Letters*, published as *The Letters of the Younger Pliny*, trans. Betty Radice. New York: Penguin Books, 1969, p. 61.
16. Martial, *Epigrams*, ed. and trans. D.R. Shackleton Bailey. 3 vols. Cambridge, MA: Harvard University Press, 1993, vol. 3, p. 301.
17. Tacitus, *Annals*, published as *Tacitus: The Annals of Imperial Rome*, trans. Michael Grant. New York: Penguin Books, 1989, p. 174.
18. The surviving volumes are numbers 1–10, covering the years 753–293 B.C., and 21–45, covering 219–167 B.C.

19. Duff, *A Literary History of Rome*, p. 464.
20. Duff, *A Literary History of Rome*, p. 473.

Chapter 2: Cato and Cicero: Fighting for Traditional Values

21. His birth name was not Cato but Marcus Porcius Priscus. He earned the name Cato later in life because of his unusual intelligence; Cato comes from the Latin word *catus,* meaning "keen intellect."
22. Plutarch, *Life of Cato,* in *Makers of Rome: Nine Lives by Plutarch,* trans. Ian Scott-Kilvert. New York: Penguin Books, 1965, p. 120.
23. Plutarch, *Cato,* pp. 123–24.
24. Plutarch, *Cato,* p. 120.
25. Plutarch, *Cato,* p. 136.
26. Plutarch, *Cato,* p. 139.
27. Anthony Everitt, *Cicero: The Life and Times of Rome's Greatest Politician.* New York: Random House, 2001, p. 23.
28. Plutarch, *Life of Cicero,* in *Fall of the Roman Republic: Six Lives by Plutarch,* trans. Rex Warner. New York: Penguin Books, 1972, p. 312.
29. Plutarch, *Cicero,* pp. 312–13.
30. Plutarch, *Cicero,* pp. 315–16.
31. Cicero, *The Brutus,* in *Cicero: On Government,* p. 326.
32. Cicero, *On Duties,* ed. M.T. Griffin and E.M. Atkins. New York: Cambridge University Press, 1991, pp. 33–34.

33. Cicero, *First Speech Against Catiline,* in *Selected Political Speeches of Cicero,* trans. Michael Grant. Baltimore, MD: Penguin Books, 1979, pp. 76–79.
34. Plutarch, *Cicero,* p. 343.

Chapter 3: Augustus and Livia: Rulers of a New Rome

35. Anthony A. Barrett, *Livia: First Lady of Imperial Rome.* New Haven, CT: Yale University Press, 2002, pp. 115–16, 119–22.
36. Suetonius, *Lives of the Twelve Caesars,* published as *The Twelve Caesars,* trans. Robert Graves, rev. Michael Grant. New York: Penguin Books, 1979, pp. 98–99.
37. Suetonius, *Twelve Caesars,* p. 57.
38. Plutarch, *Life of Antony,* in *Makers of Rome,* p. 284.
39. Plutarch, *Antony,* p. 287.
40. A.H.M. Jones, *Augustus.* New York: W.W. Norton, 1970, p. 83.
41. Augustus, *Res gestae,* in William G. Sinnegin, ed., *Sources in Western Civilization: Rome.* New York: Free Press, 1965, p. 112.
42. Quoted in Suetonius, *Twelve Caesars,* p. 69.
43. Suetonius, *Twelve Caesars,* pp. 69–71.
44. Dio Cassius, *Roman History,* published as *Roman History: The Reign of Augustus,* trans. Ian Scott-Kilvert. New York: Penguin Books, 1987, p. 255.
45. Tacitus, *Annals,* p. 41.
46. Suetonius, *Twelve Caesars,* pp. 138–39.

Chapter 4: Nero and Agrippina: The Corruption of Power

47. Anthony A. Barrett, *Agrippina: Sex, Power, and Politics in the Early Empire.* New Haven, CT: Yale University Press, 1996, p. xv.
48. Richard Holland, *Nero: The Man Behind the Myth.* Gloucestershire, England: Sutton, 2000, pp. 196–97.
49. Pliny the Elder, *Natural History,* excerpted in *Pliny the Elder: Natural History: A Selection,* trans. John H. Healy. New York: Penguin Books, 1991, p. 82.
50. Barrett, *Agrippina,* p. 86.
51. Tacitus, *Annals,* p. 262.
52. Claudius's third wife, Messalina, was a ruthless schemer and adulteress who got away with much behind his back until Claudius finally found out and divorced her in 48.
53. Suetonius, *Twelve Caesars,* pp. 217–18.
54. Suetonius, *Twelve Caesars,* p. 217.
55. Barrett, *Agrippina,* p. 156.
56. Suetonius, *Twelve Caesars,* p. 232.
57. Tacitus, *Annals,* p. 316.
58. Tacitus, *Annals,* p. 317.
59. Suetonius, *Twelve Caesars,* p. 225.
60. Tacitus, *Annals,* pp. 262–63.
61. Tacitus, *Annals,* p. 263.
62. Quoted in Suetonius, *Twelve Caesars,* p. 229.
63. Holland, *Nero,* p. 163.
64. Tacitus, *Annals,* pp. 365–66. This is perhaps the most closely studied passage from ancient literature, mainly because it is one of the few ancient sources seen as evidence for the historical reality of Jesus Christ.

Chapter 5: Pliny the Elder and Galen: The Pursuit of Knowledge

65. Pliny the Elder, *Natural History,* quoted in Michael Grant, *The World of Rome.* New York: Penguin Books, 1960, p. 93.
66. Pliny the Elder, *Natural History,* Healy translation, p. 289.
67. Pliny the Elder, *Natural History,* Healy translation, p. 5.
68. Pliny the Elder, *Natural History,* Healy translation, p. 6.
69. Pliny the Elder, *Natural History,* Healy translation, p. 5.
70. Pliny the Younger, *Letters,* pp. 87–89.
71. Pliny the Younger, *Letters,* pp. 166–68.
72. Galen, *The Affections and Errors of the Soul,* in *Galen: Selected Works,* trans. P.N. Singer. New York: Oxford University Press, 1997, pp. 119–21.
73. Galen, *The Best Doctor Is Also a Philosopher,* in Singer, *Galen,* p. 31.
74. Galen, *The Best Doctor,* in Singer, *Galen,* pp. 31–32, 34.

Chapter 6: Hadrian and Antoninus: The Good Emperors

75. Gibbon, *Decline and Fall,* vol. 1, p. 103.
76. Gibbon, *Decline and Fall,* vol. 1, pp. 37–38.

77. Royston Lambert, *Beloved of God: The Story of Hadrian and Antinous.* New York: Viking, 1984, p. 35.
78. Lambert, *Beloved of God*, p. 43.
79. *Augustan History*, published as *Lives of the Later Caesars: The First Part of the* Augustan History, *with Newly Compiled Lives of Nerva and Trajan*, trans. Anthony Birley. New York: Penguin Books, 1976, p. 85.
80. Quoted in Chris Scarre, *Chronicle of the Roman Emperors*, New York: Thames and Hudson, 1995, p. 110.
81. *Augustan History*, p. 97.
82. Michael Grant, *The Antonines: The Roman Empire in Transition.* London: Routledge, 1996, p. 12.
83. *Augustan History*, p. 97.
84. Marcus Aurelius, *Meditations*, trans. George Long, in *Great Books of the Western World*, vol. 12. Chicago: Encyclopaedia Britannica, 1952, pp. 254–55.
85. Grant, *The Antonines*, p. 21.
86. Aelius Aristides, *Roman Panegyric*, quoted in Naphtali Lewis and Meyer Reinhold, eds., *Roman Civilization, Sourcebook II: The Empire.* New York: Harper and Row, 1966, pp. 137–38.

Chapter 7: Constantine and Ambrose: Christianizing the Empire

87. Eusebius, *Ecclesiastical History*, quoted in Lewis and Reinhold, *Roman Civilization, Sourcebook II*, pp. 599–600.
88. Lactantius, *The Deaths of the Persecutors*, quoted in Michael Grant, *Constantine the Great: The Man and His Times.* New York: Scribner's, 1994, p. 21.
89. Edict of Milan, in Brian Tierney, ed., *The Middle Ages. Vol. 1: Sources of Medieval History.* New York: McGraw-Hill, 1983, pp. 20–21.
90. The other four emperors were his son, Constantius II (who ruled the east from 337 to 350 and both east and west from 350 to 361); Julian, the last pagan emperor (361–363); Jovian (363–364); and Theodosius I (ruler in the east 379–392; sole ruler 392–395).
91. Averil Cameron, *The Later Roman Empire: A.D. 284–430.* Cambridge, MA: Harvard University Press, 1993, p. 59.
92. Quoted in Tierney, *Middle Ages*, pp. 22–23.
93. Quoted in Tierney, *Middle Ages*, pp. 23–25.
94. Justo L. Gonzalez, *The Story of Christianity. Vol. 1: The Early Church to the Dawn of the Reformation.* San Francisco: Harper and Row, 1984, p. 192.

Chronology

B.C.
753
The city of Rome is founded by Romulus. (This is the traditional founding date computed and accepted by Roman scholars some seven centuries later.)

509
The leading Roman landowners throw out their last king and establish the Roman Republic.

264–241
The First Punic War occurs, in which Rome defeats the maritime empire of Carthage.

234
The noted senator and censor Cato the Elder is born.

218–201
Rome fights Carthage again in the Second Punic War, in which the Carthaginian general Hannibal crosses the Alps and invades Italy; despite enormous losses, the Romans win.

184
Cato becomes censor and begins imposing his conservative ethical views on the Roman people.

149–146
Thanks in large part to Cato's urgings, Rome annihilates Carthage in the Third Punic War.

106
Cicero, orator, statesman, prolific writer, and the last great champion of the Republic, is born.

70
Virgil, widely viewed as Rome's greatest poet, is born.

63
Cicero is elected consul; he exposes and crushes a conspiracy to kill the consuls and seize control of the government; Octavian, Julius Caesar's great-nephew and later adopted son, is born.

ca. 59
Livy, one of Rome's greatest historians, is born.

44
After declaring himself "dictator for life," Caesar is assassinated by a group of senators; Cicero publishes one of his greatest works, *On Duties*.

43
Octavian joins forces with military generals Mark Antony and Marcus Lepidus in an alliance known as the Second Triumvirate; the triumvirs murder many of their political enemies, including Cicero.

39
Octavian meets Livia, his future wife and the future empress of Rome.

31

Octavian defeats Antony and Egypt's Queen Cleopatra at Actium (in western Greece) and gains firm control of the Mediterranean world.

ca. 30 B.C.–A.D. 180

During the so called Pax Romana ("Roman peace"), the Mediterranean world under the first several Roman emperors enjoys relative peace and prosperity.

27

The Senate gives Octavian the title of Augustus ("the revered one") and he becomes, in effect, Rome's first emperor.

19

Virgil dies; his epic poem, the *Aeneid,* is published posthumously.

A.D.
6

Augustus establishes a fire-fighting force (the *vigiles*) to protect the Roman capital.

14

Augustus dies, plunging the Roman people into a period of deep mourning; he is succeeded by Livia's son, Tiberius.

15

Agrippina the Younger, future sister, wife, and mother of Roman emperors, is born.

ca. 17

Livy dies.

23

The great Roman encyclopedist Pliny the Elder is born.

29

Livia dies.

37

Agrippina's brother Caligula becomes the third emperor; her son, Nero, is born.

54

Agrippina poisons her husband, the emperor Claudius, and Nero ascends the throne.

59

Nero has Agrippina killed.

64

A great fire ravages large sections of Rome; Nero blames the disaster on local Christians and executes many of them.

68

The army, Senate, and people turn on Nero, who commits suicide.

ca. 71–79

Pliny the Elder writes his massive *Natural History.*

76

The future emperor Hadrian is born.

79

The volcano Mt. Vesuvius erupts, burying the Italian towns of Pompeii and Herculaneum; Pliny the Elder dies while observing the disaster up close.

86

The future emperor Antoninus Pius is born.

98

Trajan, Hadrian's adoptive father, becomes emperor; under Trajan, the Empire reaches its greatest size and power.

110

Antoninus Pius marries Faustina the Elder.

117
Trajan dies and Hadrian succeeds him.

122
Hadrian visits Britain and plans the construction of the massive defensive wall that will bear his name.

ca. 130
Galen, Rome's foremost medical practitioner, is born.

138
Hadrian dies and is succeeded by his adopted son, Antoninus Pius.

161
Antoninus dies and his own adopted son, Marcus Aurelius, becomes emperor.

180
Marcus Aurelius dies, marking the end of the Pax Romana era and the beginning of Rome's steady slide into economic and political crisis.

ca. 200
Galen dies.

235–284
The Empire suffers under the strain of terrible political upheaval and civil strife, prompting later historians to call this period "the Anarchy."

ca. 273
Future emperor Constantine I is born.

284
Diocletian ascends the throne and initiates sweeping political, economic, and social reforms, in effect reconstructing the Empire under a new blueprint. (Modern histori-

ans often call this new realm the Later Empire.)

303
Diocletian and his lieutenant, Galerius, launch the largest Christian persecution in Roman history.

306
Constantine becomes one of the four rulers of the Empire.

312
Constantine defeats his chief rival, Maxentius, at Rome's Milvian Bridge.

313
Constantine and his eastern colleague, Licinius, issue the so-called Edict of Milan, granting religious toleration to the formerly hated and persecuted Christians.

324
Constantine defeats Licinius, becoming sole ruler of the Roman realm.

330
Constantine founds the city of Constantinople on the Bosporus Strait, making it the capital of the eastern section of the Empire.

337
Constantine dies; he converts to Christianity on his deathbed.

ca. 340
Ambrose, future bishop of Milan, is born.

391
At the urging of Christian leaders, especially Ambrose, the emperor Theodosius I closes the pagan temples, demolishing some and turning others into museums. In less than

a century, Christianity has become the Empire's official religion.

395

The last emperor to rule both western and eastern Rome, Theodosius, dies and leaves his young sons, Honorius and Arcadius, in charge of a divided realm.

397

Ambrose dies.

476

A German-born Roman general deposes the young emperor Romulus Augustulus, and no new emperor takes his place. Historians mark this event as the fall of the western Roman realm, although the succession of Roman emperors continues in the eastern realm, which steadily evolves into the Byzantine Empire.

For Further Reading

Books

Peter Chrisp, *The Roman Emperor*. New York: Peter Bedrick Books, 1999. The powers, duties, and life of a typical Roman emperor are covered in this attractively mounted volume aimed at junior high school readers.

Phil R. Cox and Annabel Spenceley, *Who Were the Romans?* Boston: EDC, 1994. An impressive, well-illustrated introduction to the Romans, presented in a question-and-answer format.

John Haaren et al., *Famous Men of Rome*. Lebanon, TN: Greenleaf Press, 1989. This is a reprint of an older but still relevant and widely read book on important Roman figures. A useful study guide for the book is also available from the same publisher.

Anthony Marks and Graham Tingay, *The Romans*. London: Usborne, 1990. An excellent summary of the main aspects of Roman history, life, and arts, supported by hundreds of beautiful and accurate drawings reconstructing Roman times. Aimed at basic readers but highly recommended for anyone interested in Roman civilization.

Anthony Masters, *Roman Myths and Legends*. New York: Peter Bedrick Books, 2000. A worthwhile general overview of some of the basic Roman myths, including the founding of Rome by Romulus.

Don Nardo, *Rulers of Ancient Rome*. San Diego: Lucent Books, 1999. This informative volume of multiple biographies covers the lives and exploits of major Roman leaders, including Fabius, Marius, Caesar, Cicero, Augustus, Nero, Constantine, and Justinian.

Richard Platt, *Julius Caesar: Great Dictator of Rome*. London: Dorling Kindersley, 2001. This beautifully illustrated volume is an excellent introduction to one of the greatest Roman figures; also features a large, colorful fold-out section.

Judith Simpson, *Ancient Rome*. New York: Time-Life Books, 1997. One of Time-Life's library of picture books about the ancient world, this one is beautifully illustrated with attractive and appropriate photographs and paintings. The general but well-written text is aimed at intermediate young readers.

Websites

Battle at the Milvian Bridge, Wikipedia Encyclopedia, 2003. www.wiki pedia.org. A useful site that gives the background of the famous battle in which the emperor Constantine defeated his rival using a Christian symbol as his battle emblem. Contains many links to related subjects.

Cicero (ca.106–43 B.C.), Internet Encyclopedia of Philosophy, 2001. www.utm.edu. An excellent, easy-to-read overview of the great Roman orator's life, influence, and works.

Online Encyclopedia of the Roman Emperors, compiled by a consortium of scholars, 2002. www.romanemper ors.org. Lists all of the Roman emperors, each with a link to a detailed, informative biography of his life and deeds. Highly recommended.

Prima Porta: Villa of Livia, Classical Archaeology and Ancient History, Uppsala University, 2000. www.arke ologi.uu. This colorful and informative site provides a history and virtual tour, as well as a chronicle of excavations, at the primary villa of Augustus's wife and empress, Livia.

Major Works Consulted

Ancient Sources

Ambrose, *Letters,* published as *Letters of St. Ambrose.* Trans. H. De Romestin. New York: Christian Literature, 1896.

Ammianus Marcellinus, *History,* published as *The Later Roman Empire, A.D. 354–378.* Trans. and ed. Walter Hamilton. New York: Penguin Books, 1986.

Appian, *Roman History.* Trans. Horace White. Cambridge, MA: Harvard University Press, 1964; and excerpted in *Appian: The Civil Wars.* Trans. John Carter. New York: Penguin Books, 1996.

Augustan History, published as *Lives of the Later Caesars: The First Part of the Augustan History, with Newly Compiled Lives of Nerva and Trajan.* Trans. Anthony Birley. New York: Penguin Books, 1976.

Leon Bernard and Theodore B. Hodges, eds., *Readings in European History.* New York: Macmillan, 1958.

Cato, *On Agriculture.* Trans. Ernest Brehaut. New York: Columbia University Press, 1933.

Cicero, selected works in *Cicero: Murder Trials.* Trans. Michael Grant. New York: Penguin Books, 1990; *Cicero: On Government.* Trans. Michael Grant. New York: Penguin Books, 1993; *On Duties.* Ed. M.T. Griffin and E.M. Atkins. New York: Cambridge University Press, 1991; *Letters to Atticus.* Trans. E.O. Winstedt. 3 vols. Cambridge, MA: Harvard University Press, 1961; *Letters to His Friends.* Trans. W. Glynn Williams. 3 vols. Cambridge, MA: Harvard University Press, 1965; and *Selected Political Speeches of Cicero.* Trans. Michael Grant. Baltimore, MD: Penguin Books, 1979.

Dio Cassius, *Roman History,* published as *Roman History: The Reign of Augustus.* Trans. Ian Scott-Kilvert. New York: Penguin Books, 1987; and summarized in Xiphilinus, *Epitome.* Ed. Ernest Cary. Cambridge, MA: Harvard University Press, 1927.

Aelius Donatus, *Life of Virgil.* Trans. David Wilson-Okamura. 1996. http://virgil.org.

Eusebius, *Ecclesiastical History.* Trans. Roy J. Deferrari. 2 vols. Washington, DC: Catholic University of America Press, 1955; and *Life of Constantine.* Trans. E.C. Richardson. New York: Christian Literature, 1890.

Galen, various works in *Galen: Selected Works.* Trans. P.N. Singer. New York: Oxford University Press, 1997.

Naphtali Lewis and Meyer Reinhold, eds., *Roman Civilization, Sourcebook I: The Republic,* and *Roman Civilization, Sourcebook II: The Empire.* Both New York: Harper and Row, 1966.

Livy, *The History of Rome from Its Foundation,* books 1–5 published as *Livy: The Early History of Rome.* Trans. Aubrey de Sélincourt. New York: Penguin Books, 1960; books 21–30 published as *Livy: The War with Hannibal.* Trans. Aubrey de Sélincourt. New York: Penguin Books, 1972; books 31–45 published as *Livy: Rome and the Mediterranean.* Trans. Henry Bettenson. New York: Penguin Books, 1976. Also, various books excerpted in *Livy, Vol. 2.* Trans. Canon Roberts. New York: E.P. Dutton, 1912.

Marcus Aurelius, *Meditations.* Trans. George Long. In *Great Books of the Western World.* Vol. 12. Chicago: Encyclopaedia Britannica, 1952.

Martial, *Epigrams.* Ed. and trans. D.R. Shackleton Bailey. 3 vols. Cambridge, MA: Harvard University Press, 1993.

Pliny the Elder, *Natural History.* Trans. H. Rackham. 10 vols. Cambridge, MA: Harvard University Press, 1967; and excerpted in *Pliny the Elder: Natural History: A Selection.* Trans. John H. Healy. New York: Penguin Books, 1991.

Pliny the Younger, *Letters.* Trans. William Melmouth. 2 vols. Cambridge, MA: Harvard University Press, 1961; also published as *The Letters of the Younger Pliny.* Trans. Betty Radice. New York: Penguin Books, 1969.

Plutarch, *Parallel Lives,* published complete as *Lives of the Noble Grecians and Romans.* Trans. John Dryden. New York: Random House, 1932; also excerpted in *The Age of Alexander: Nine Greek Lives by Plutarch.* Trans. Ian Scott-Kilvert. New York: Penguin Books, 1973; *Fall of the Roman Republic: Six Lives by Plutarch.* Trans. Rex Warner. New York: Penguin Books, 1972; and *Makers of Rome: Nine Lives by Plutarch.* Trans. Ian Scott-Kilvert. New York: Penguin Books, 1965.

Sallust, *Works.* Trans. J.C. Rolfe. New York: Cambridge University Press, 1965; also, *Sallust: The Jugurthine War/The Conspiracy of Catiline.* Trans. S.A. Handford. New York: Penguin Books, 1988.

Seneca, *Moral Epistles.* Trans. Richard M. Gummere. 3 vols. Cambridge, MA: Harvard University Press, 1961; *Moral Essays.* Trans. John W. Basore. 3 vols. Cambridge, MA: Harvard University Press, 1963; and assorted works collected in *The Stoic Philosophy of Seneca.* Trans. and ed. Moses Hadas. New York: W.W. Norton, 1958; and *Seneca: Dialogues and Letters.* Trans. and ed. C.D.N. Costa. New York: Penguin Books, 1997.

Jo-Ann Shelton, ed., *As the Romans Did: A Sourcebook in Roman Social History.* New York: Oxford University Press, 1988.

William G. Sinnegin, ed., *Sources in Western Civilization: Rome.* New York: Free Press, 1965.

Suetonius, *Lives of the Twelve Caesars*, published as *The Twelve Caesars*. Trans. Robert Graves. Rev. Michael Grant. New York: Penguin Books, 1979.

Tacitus, *Annals*, published as *Tacitus: The Annals of Imperial Rome*. Trans. Michael Grant. New York: Penguin Books, 1989.

Brian Tierney, ed., *The Middle Ages. Vol. 1: Sources of Medieval History*. New York: McGraw-Hill, 1983.

Virgil, *Aeneid*. Trans. Patric Dickinson. New York: New American Library, 1961; also, *Aeneid*. Trans. David West. New York: Penguin, 1990; also, *Works*. Trans. H. Rushton Fairclough. 2 vols. Cambridge, MA: Harvard University Press, 1967.

Modern Sources

Anthony A. Barrett, *Agrippina: Sex, Power, and Politics in the Early Empire*. New Haven, CT: Yale University Press, 1996. An impressive piece of scholarship, this study of Nero's mother and her influence on the imperial court and government makes the point that, while she was scheming and ambitious, she also had some positive traits that posterity has come to forget or ignore. Highly recommended.

———, *Livia: First Lady of Imperial Rome*. New Haven, CT: Yale University Press, 2002. Another excellent historical study by Barrett, this one is the first full-length book in English about Livia, Augustus's wife and perhaps the most influential woman in Roman history.

Averil Cameron, *The Later Roman Empire: A.D. 284–430*. Cambridge, MA: Harvard University Press, 1993. Contains excellent general, up-to-date summaries of Diocletian's administrative and other reforms and Constantine's reforms, including his acceptance of Christianity.

F.R. Cowell, *Cicero and the Roman Republic*. Baltimore, MD: Penguin Books, 1967. A very detailed and insightful analysis of the late Republic, its leaders (Cicero, Caesar, and Octavian prominent among them), and the problems that led to its collapse. Very highly recommended.

Michael Crawford, *The Roman Republic*. Cambridge, MA: Harvard University Press, 1993. This is one of the best available overviews of the Republic, offering various insights into the nature of the political, cultural, and intellectual forces that shaped the decisions of Roman leaders, including Caesar, Cicero, and Octavian.

Anthony Everitt, *Cicero: The Life and Times of Rome's Greatest Politician*. New York: Random House, 2001. A fine new telling of Cicero's deeds, this one uses the great man's own letters and other ancient sources to weave an absorbing panorama of the political, military, and social currents of Rome in the first century B.C. Highly recommended.

John B. Firth, *Augustus Caesar and the Organization of the Empire of Rome*. Freeport, NY: Books for the Libraries

Press, 1972. Beginning with Caesar's assassination in 44 B.C., this is a detailed, thoughtful telling of the final years of the Republic, including Octavian's rise to power during the civil wars and his ascendancy as Augustus, the first Roman emperor.

Michael Grant, *The Antonines: The Roman Empire in Transition*. London: Routledge, 1996. A penetrating, informative look at the Antonines—Antoninus Pius, Marcus Aurelius, Lucius Verus, and Commodus—and how they ruled the Empire when it was moving from the unbridled prosperity of the Pax Romana toward a less stable era.

———, *Constantine the Great: The Man and His Times*. New York: Scribner's, 1994. A very fine study of Constantine, his achievements (Christianity, Constantinople, etc.), and his impact on the Roman Empire and later ages.

———, *History of Rome*. New York: Scribner's, 1978. Comprehensive, insightful, and well written, this is one of the best available general overviews of Roman civilization from its founding to its fall.

Miriam T. Griffin, *Nero: The End of a Dynasty*. New Haven, CT: Yale University Press, 1984. Griffin, a distinguished scholar of Somerville College, Oxford, delivers a commendable, readable, very well documented study of one of the most colorful and reviled of Rome's leaders. Highly recommended.

Richard Holland, *Nero: The Man Behind the Myth*. Gloucestershire, England: Sutton, 2000. A fine recent piece of scholarship that shows Nero as a more complex and interesting character than he is usually portrayed.

A.H.M. Jones, *Augustus*. New York: W.W. Norton, 1970. Like all Jones's works, this one presents all the relevant facts within a framework of masterful analysis. The author's central point is that, for good or ill, Augustus's creation of the Principate was a major political achievement that had a lasting impact on Roman society.

———, *Constantine and the Conversion of Europe*. Toronto: University of Toronto Press, 1978. A superior general overview of Constantine's world and his influence, particularly in the area of religion, by one of the twentieth century's greatest Roman scholars.

Royston Lambert, *Beloved of God: The Story of Hadrian and Antinous*. New York: Viking, 1984. A fascinating indepth study of the emperor Hadrian and his lover, Antinous. Captures the atmosphere, especially the religious and artistic trends, of the early-second-century Roman world.

Thomas N. Mitchell, *Cicero: The Senior Statesman*. New Haven, CT: Yale University Press, 1991. An informative, up-to-date study of the great politician, orator, writer, courageous champion of the disintegrating

Republic, and one of the most important and influential literary figures in Western history.

Chris Scarre, *Chronicle of the Roman Emperors*. New York: Thames and Hudson, 1995. A well-written general overview of the emperors, supplemented by numerous primary-source materials and useful time lines.

P.G. Walsh, *Livy: His Historical Aims and Methods*. New York: Cambridge University Press, 1967. An in-depth study of Livy, his writings, his methods, and his moral and philosophical attitudes.

Additional Works Consulted

Lesley Adkins and Roy A. Adkins, *Handbook to Life in Ancient Rome.* New York: Facts On File, 1994.

Timothy D. Barnes, *Constantine and Eusebius.* Cambridge, MA: Harvard University Press, 1981.

Arthur E.R. Boak, *A History of Rome to 565 A.D.* New York: Macmillan, 1943.

John Buchan, *Augustus.* London: Hodder and Stoughton, 1937.

Matthew Bunson, *A Dictionary of the Roman Empire.* Oxford, England: Oxford University Press, 1991.

Owen Chadwick, *A History of Christianity.* New York: St. Martin's Press, 1995.

J. Wight Duff, *A Literary History of Rome, from the Origins to the Close of the Golden Age.* New York: Barnes and Noble, 1960.

Charles Freeman, *Egypt, Greece, and Rome: Civilizations of the Ancient Mediterranean.* Oxford, England: Oxford University Press, 1996.

Edward Gibbon, *The Decline and Fall of the Roman Empire.* Ed. David Womersley. 3 vols. New York: Penguin Books, 1994.

Justo L. Gonzalez, *The Story of Christianity. Vol. 1: The Early Church to the Dawn of the Reformation.* San Francisco: Harper and Row, 1984.

Michael Grant, *Julius Caesar.* New York: M. Evens, 1992.

——, *The Roman Emperors.* New York: Barnes and Noble, 1997.

——, *The World of Rome.* New York: Penguin Books, 1960.

Ramon L. Jimenez, *Caesar Against Rome: The Great Roman Civil War.* London: Praeger, 2000.

A.H.M. Jones, *The Decline of the Ancient World.* London: Longman Group, 1966.

Marjorie Lightman and Benjamin Lightman, *Biographical Dictionary of Ancient Greek and Roman Women.* New York: Facts On File, 2000.

Ramsay MacMullen, *Christianizing the Roman Empire, A.D. 100–400.* New Haven, CT: Yale University Press, 1984.

——, *Constantine.* New York: Dial Press, 1969.

——, *Roman Government's Response to Crisis: A.D. 235–337.* New Haven, CT: Yale University Press, 1976.

Neil B. McLynn, *Ambrose of Milan: Church and Court in a Christian Capital.* Berkeley: University of California Press, 1994.

Torsten Petersson, *Cicero: A Biography.* New York: Biblo and Tannen, 1963.

John C. Rolfe, *Cicero and His Influence.* New York: Cooper Square, 1963.

Henry T. Rowell, *Rome in the Augustan Age*. Norman: University of Oklahoma Press, 1962.

Chester G. Starr, *Civilization and the Caesars: The Intellectual Revolution in the Roman Empire*. New York: W.W. Norton, 1965.

———, *A History of the Ancient World*. New York: Oxford University Press, 1991.

Lily Ross Taylor, *Party Politics in the Age of Caesar*. Berkeley and Los Angeles: University of California Press, 1968.

L.P. Wilkinson, *The Roman Experience*. Lanham, MD: University Press of America, 1974.

Garry Wills, ed., *Roman Culture: Weapons and the Man*. New York: George Braziller, 1966.

Index

Picture Credits

About the Author

Classical historian Don Nardo has published many volumes about ancient Roman history and culture, including *The Punic Wars, The Age of Augustus, A Travel Guide to Ancient Rome, Life of a Roman Gladiator,* and Greenhaven Press's massive *Encyclopedia of Greek and Roman Mythology.* Mr. Nardo also writes screenplays and teleplays and composes music. He lives in Massachusetts with his wife, Christine.